THE BEST-LAID PLANS

THE
BEST-LAID
PLANS

*America's Juvenile
Court Experiment*

ELLEN RYERSON

Hill and Wang • New York
A division of Farrar, Straus and Giroux

Copyright © 1978 by Ellen Ryerson
All rights reserved
Published simultaneously in Canada
by McGraw-Hill Ryerson Ltd., Toronto
Printed in the United States of America
Designed by Paula Wiener

Library of Congress Cataloging in Publication Data
Ryerson, Ellen. The best-laid plans.
  Includes bibliographical references and index.
    1. Juvenile courts—United States—History.
I. Title.
KF9794.R9   345'.73'08   78-4643

To
DAVID S. LOVEJOY

ACKNOWLEDGMENTS

I wish to thank a number of people for their criticism, comments, and assistance during my work on this study. John Morton Blum supervised, and André Ryerson read critically the dissertation in which it began. Frederick Errington, Theodore Greene, Allen Guttmann, and John William Ward each read and commented on one of several stages it has passed through since; their generous attention to the work of a colleague is one of many things I remember with pleasure and gratitude about my years at Amherst College.

Dean Harry H. Wellington of Yale Law School has helped me find the time to complete the manuscript. Martha Kootz, my secretary, typed it with the skill, good judgment, and graciousness that she brings to all her work.

E. R.
New Haven, 1977

CONTENTS

THE BEST-LAID PLANS

INTRODUCTION

In 1899, the Illinois legislature passed a law creating a new and separate court to resolve legal problems concerning dependent, neglected, and delinquent children. The hallmarks of its approach were relatively few and simple: children—even children who broke the criminal law—differed from adults. They required not only separate but different treatment before the law. The state, acting through the juvenile court, must treat children not as responsible moral agents subject to the condemnation of the community but as wards in need of care. A special court for children should be of civil jurisdiction, with flexible procedures adapted to diagnosing and preventing as well as to curing delinquency.

During the next two decades almost all the states imitated, more or less precisely, the Illinois legislature. The juvenile court became the dominant institution in the juvenile justice system for the twentieth century.

The subject of this book narrowly conceived is the juvenile court—its conception, the assumptions upon which it was based, and its fate as a reform idea. More broadly and indirectly, the subject is the degree to which the juvenile court represented a more general perception of and approach to social problems, and to which its fate exemplifies changes in American perceptions of and solutions to similar problems. For the subject narrowly conceived, it might be enough to set the juvenile court in the history of reform efforts in juvenile justice and corrections. But, for the subject broadly conceived, it is also necessary to set the court in its historical period.

For the latter, one cannot begin in 1899: that was an important year in the history of the juvenile court movement, but it was not the beginning. A bill similar to the one that passed in 1899 had failed in 1891, and before the Illinois legislation authorized the creation of a juvenile court, at least one judge elsewhere in the nation was experimenting with similar forms without legislative authorization. The idea originated in the early 1890's; its spread and refinement occurred largely in the first two decades of the twentieth century. The period from the conception of the idea of a separate court for children to its virtual triumph as a means for dealing with juveniles extends, then, from the early 1890's to the end of the second decade of the twentieth century, and largely coincides with the period historians have called the progressive era.

One asks for trouble by suggesting that an institution bears the imprint of a certain period—more trouble even than the considerable one of finding and naming the qualities which distinguish one block of time from another. One asks for particular trouble in suggesting that the connection between the juvenile court and the progressive era is more than coincidence and concatenation—all the trouble of distinguishing the progressive era from its past and future, and all that of distinguishing the juvenile court movement from the efforts in juvenile justice reform which preceded it. The trouble is serious: the idea of the juvenile court included some elements which go back as far as Jacksonian America and further, across both time and place. Further, the historiography of the progressive era is a virtual thicket of questions in which one risks getting lost. One question is whether the movement for which it is named was peopled by an old middle class acting out status frustrations, or by a new middle class acting out its professional ambitions, or by a business elite seeking a predictable environment in which to pursue its own interests.[1] A variant of the question is whether progressivism was a movement of humanitarian reform that failed or a movement of capitalist conservatism that succeeded. Did the many different people who called themselves progressives leave us with a term that connotes something in particular or nothing at all?[2] These are questions which I do not wish to engage directly.

It will do, I hope, to say that I find something distinctive in the problems which Americans faced at the end of the nineteenth century and the beginning of the twentieth, even if the distinction is more one of scale than of kind. I find something even more distinctive in the perception of those problems and responses to them. Finally, I believe that the juvenile court movement, though it built upon some ideas which had fairly long histories and attacked a problem with an endless history, did so in a style which makes its location in the progressive period more than a coincidence. But this is not an unlimited claim for the uniqueness of the juvenile court or for the distinctiveness of the progressive era, or for an uncomplicated causal relationship between them. Perhaps the more one learns the more one is apt to agree that there is nothing new under the sun. Nonetheless, distinctions even within a pattern of continuity may be worth making.

Most if not all the problems to which progressivism responded grew out of the development of industrial capitalism, and particularly out of the acceleration of that development in the nineteenth century. Between the end of the Civil War and the beginning of the twentieth century, the United States became the leading agricultural and industrial producer in the world. Most if not all of the problems emanating from economic development had troubled previous generations. Many of them became both more acute and more visible with the rise of American cities.

As Richard Hofstadter points out in *The Age of Reform,* the vast growth of cities after the Civil War deeply unsettled habitually rural Americans by what seemed "not merely a new social form or way of life, but a strange threat to civilization itself."[3] Between 1880 and 1910 the number of people living in American cities trebled from 15 million to 45 million, while the total population less than doubled. At the beginning of this period, one third of the national population was urban; at the end almost one half, or 49 percent, lived in cities. Between 1870 and 1900 Chicago grew from a population of 250,000 to one of nearly 1,700,000. This growth put terrible strains upon systems which delivered crucial public utilities and services like transportation, police protection, sewage disposal, and garbage collection. Political corruption distorted the process by which these systems might efficiently have met the growing demand. But it was not the sheer size of cities which was alarming; it was also the proportion of their populations which was poor and foreign.

Robert Bremner tells us that Americans first "discovered" poverty in the cities of the early nineteenth century in the wake of the panics of 1819 and 1837: they then began to write of the revolting living conditions of the urban poor. The panic of 1893 and the severe depression which followed it, with an unemployment rate of 20 percent, again reminded Americans of the squalor and poverty of much of urban life. "Never," Bremner says, "before the closing decade of the nineteenth century had [the] shadow [of unemployment] hung so heavily over so many men and women."[4]

The hazard of unemployment was not the only one facing the industrial workers. The persistent problems of long working hours and injuries and deaths due to dangerous working conditions also plagued them. The struggle to organize unions to force changes in these conditions punctuated the 1890's with a startling number of strikes and evoked a good deal of violence. The most famous and disturbing of these industrial conflicts took place between workers and managers of the Homestead plant of Carnegie Steel in 1892 and the Pullman Company in 1894. But these were only the most alarming among the many strikes which involved a record 750,000 workers in the depression years.[5]

The urban unemployed were joined during the depression by migrants from the countryside, where the number of farms was declining and where farm tenancy was increasing as a result of collapsing prices for agricultural produce. They were also joined by immigrants more alien in their origins and eventually more threatening in their numbers than the United States had ever encountered. From 1881 to 1890, the proportion of the entering population that came from Southern and Eastern rather than Northern Europe amounted to something under 20 percent. In the nineties, it climbed to 52 percent, and between 1901 and 1910, to 74 percent. At the same time, the number of people entering the United States yearly more than doubled, and the problem of assimilation took on, simultaneously, new qualitative and quantitative dimensions.

Outside the cities there were other problems. The growing population in the late nineteenth century was rapidly filling the continent. Between 1607 and 1870, 400 million acres of land were occupied. In the next thirty years alone, as many acres were occupied, and more. Millions of acres had gone in grants to the railroads. In 1900 some 500 million acres remained open to settlement under the land laws, but much of this was of questionable use in agricultural production due to limited rainfall. Only if irrigated could even 100 million of those acres be brought under cultivation.[6] While some 26 million acres of public land had been withdrawn from private sale, the natural resources in timber, minerals, and water on these lands were not well protected from private exploitation. Continued depletion of natural resources could turn the potential of abundance to serious scarcity.

While the rise of corporate industrial capitalism might be implicated only indirectly in some of the problems in the cities and countryside, the conduct of corporate economic life presented a direct cause for concern. The cry against concentration of economic power may have been louder and clearer in the Jacksonian and Populist periods, but the process of economic consolidation had gone much further when the progressives turned their attention to it. During the second half of the nineteenth century, businessmen had devised a number of tools with which to control their markets. Pools, trusts, holding companies, interlocking directorates threatened small producers and consumers even if they frustrated big businessmen by their ineffectiveness. The trust as a monopolistic prac-

tice fell to the combined pressures of the panic of 1893 and
the threat of state and federal legislation against combinations
in restraint of trade. But the Supreme Court in its 1895 decision in *U.S. v. E. C. Knight Co.* interpreted the Sherman
Antitrust Act to apply only to commerce, and not to production. The decision put intrastate manufacturing monopolies
beyond the reach of federal antitrust legislation and encouraged a new spate of industrial consolidation. In 1901, the
United States Steel Company was born of J. P. Morgan's
efforts to combine 60 percent of the iron and steel producers
in one corporation capitalized at over a billion dollars. By
1904, the Standard Oil Company, organized in 1879, refined
more than 84 percent of American crude oil and carried in its
pipelines over 90 percent. In 1904, the financial empires of
J. P. Morgan and John D. Rockefeller dominated Wall Street;
in 1907, they too began a merger. In the heavily consolidated
railroad industry, differential rates and rebates favored major
shippers and discriminated against others. Small-scale producers felt aggrieved by the necessity to compete in an
economy dominated by giant corporations; consumers suffered
from the unregulated marketing of food produced under un-
sanitary conditions and of drugs of uncertain origin and effectiveness.

As all of these problems took on such scale that individual
and private efforts to deal with them seemed increasingly
futile, the central issue became what, if anything, should government do to control and guide processes which had been
left largely to run their own course. From social Darwinists,
who continued to take the lesson from nature that the health
of society depended upon struggle for survival among people
and institutions, the answer came that government should do
nothing. But from other quarters came increasingly clear demands for the state to take responsibility for controlling
economic life and ameliorating social conditions.

One response to social and economic problems was to
modify the political system to make it more responsive to
popular control. During the late 1890's and early twentieth
century, such devices as the short ballot, the direct primary

system, popular initiatives of and referenda on legislation, and recall of elected officials seemed to invite increasingly popular participation in the political process.

I believe, however, with others, that another kind of response better characterizes the progressive era. As political reform made popular participation in some political decisions more direct, other reforms took a host of issues out of the political arena and put them into the hands of experts for their continuous supervision without pressure from the political process.[7]

Perhaps the first set of problems to receive the attention of reformers were those presented by the inadequacy of urban services and the corruption of urban government, which, reformers believed, prevented the rational and economical provision of those services. Although the progressive era is usually dated from the return of prosperity in the late 1890's, Melvin Holli locates the beginnings of an urban reform movement in the depression itself.[8] Holli describes two somewhat divergent urban reform responses in the progressive period. One, which he calls the "social reform" tradition, located the source of political corruption in utility companies and other business organizations which used the political system to secure favors at the expense of city dwellers, particularly the poor. Reformers in this tradition concentrated on eliminating such influence in order to lower the costs of services, to provide some amenities such as public baths and playgrounds in the poorer areas of the city, and to redistribute the tax burden. They seem to have concentrated on the delivery of valued services and amenities. One might include with this tradition, though Holli does not, the efforts of a variety of private organizations to attend to the needs of immigrants and other poor people through settlement houses and other quasi-missionary endeavors. These organizations, too, without banishing moralism altogether from the analysis of poverty, moved with the social reform tradition to a view of poverty which pictured the poor more as victims of economic forces beyond their control than as the victims of their own moral and social inadequacy.

The second urban reform response Holli calls the "structural reform" tradition. This wing of urban reform located the source of political failings, not in the influence of profit-seeking businessmen, but in the organization of the city into wards where immigrants wielded undue political influence over politicians dependent upon them for reelection. The structural reformers concentrated on devising a form of city administration immune to popular pressure from immigrants and the poor, and controlled by professional managers and experts elected at large or, preferably, appointed through a civil service system. Holli finds that the structural school of urban reform, with its emphasis on scientific management and efficiency, became dominant by the end of the progressive era in the form of city-commissioner and city-manager systems of government.

Prosperity returned in the late 1890's, but the desire to take control of socioeconomic and political processes remained, and reform interest extended beyond the cities to state and federal legislatures. Some of the efforts on the state and national levels, like the social reform tradition's response to urban problems, seem to have been concentrated on direct delivery of moderate substantive change. But it seems more typical of progressive responses to have concentrated upon the creation of machinery for the supervision and regulation of economic activity by experts and nonpartisan commissions which were often guided in their work only by vague mandates.

State legislators made efforts to improve the health and safety of industrial workers by establishing systems of factory inspection. To do something for the victims of dangerous industrial production methods, Maryland passed a workmen's compensation law in 1902 which was much imitated. Illinois passed the first program of public assistance to mothers of dependent children in 1911. In 1912, the Massachusetts legislature created a commission to establish minimum wages for women and children and thus to put a floor under competition in the labor market which threatened to drive wages down. Many states passed laws limiting the use of child labor.

In response to rate discrimination in the railroad industry,

Congress passed the Elkins Act of 1903 and the Hepburn Act
of 1906 to strengthen the capacity of the Interstate Commerce
Commission to enforce "just and reasonable rates." For the
problem of the boom-and-bust business cycle, the Owen-Glass
Act of 1914 created a Federal Reserve Board of appointed
members to supervise the operations of a system of district
banks, and to control the elasticity of the currency by raising
and lowering rediscount rates. To deal with unfair competition in interstate commerce, the Federal Trade Commission
Act created in 1914 a commission with bipartisan membership
to investigate business practices and issue cease-and-desist
orders to prevent such unfair practices as trade boycotts and
combinations for maintaining resale prices. The other major
piece of legislation added to this regulatory system in the progressive period was the Clayton Act, also passed in 1914. The
Clayton Act specified certain illegal practices—price discrimi-
nations tending to create monopoly, interlocking directorates
in aggregations capitalized at $1 million or more, and pur-
chases of stocks which diminished competition among them—
which could be controlled either by cease-and-desist orders
from the Federal Trade Commission or by court injunctions.
While there were some well-publicized prosecutions of industrial combinations during the progressive period, the record
indicates an inclination to regulate large-scale economic enterprise rather than to reduce the size of industrial combinations.

   The preference for flexible, expert, continuous regulation
rather than discouragement or prohibition of economic activity also characterized the conservation movement. Indeed,
Samuel Hays used the conservation effort as a case study to
establish his thesis that progressivism above all stood for a
drastic change in the location of political power from legislative to administrative agencies and out of electoral politics.[9]
The Newlands Reclamation Act of 1902 was the first and last
major piece of legislation in the period concerned with conservation. This act devoted most of the proceeds of public-
land sales in the West and Southwest to the irrigation of arid
lands. Upon it and upon the preexisting power of the executive to withdraw land from private sale into federal reserves,

Gifford Pinchot, chief forester of the U.S. Forest Service, built an organization of experts to manage the national domain. The charging of fees and the issuance of permits for grazing and licenses for hydroelectric development provided the tools of their administration; the rational exploitation of natural resources their aim.

It was not for want of trying that the progressive generation inaugurated no system for dealing with the immigration problem until the end of the period. Efforts to control somewhat the nature of immigration began in the 1880's. In 1882 a federal law excluded criminals, paupers, the insane, and other undesirables, and imposed a head tax; in 1885 another law prohibited the importation of contract labor except in the professions, skilled trades, and domestic service; in 1903 another measure provided for inspection of immigrants in European ports and the deportation of people who entered the country illegally. But the scale and nature of the new immigration demanded new tools, and the one which was repeatedly suggested in the period was the literacy test. The first literacy-test legislation passed by Congress was vetoed by Cleveland in 1896, the second by Taft in 1913, the third and fourth by Wilson in 1915 and 1917. In 1917 the Congress finally overrode a presidential veto and inaugurated an era of serious immigration restriction. In the meantime, efforts to assimilate those who could not be kept out fell to the public schools and to those private individuals who established settlement houses in the cities.

To contend with the scale and severity of the problems they confronted, the progressive generation mustered remarkable energy and optimism. One author has written that nothing is more characteristic of the progressive era than the facility with which "intellectuals uncovered social theories that overcame their uneasiness about the rapidly changing environment. . . . They generally found comfortable answers to their questions and never doubted that the problems had solutions."[10] Their typical solutions had a strong procedural cast, but their emphasis upon efficiency and administration did not exclude moral discourse. The quest for solutions took place in the context of what appeared a moral drama to the participants and to many of the historians who first wrote about them.[11] If, as now seems certain, the drama was not predominantly a conflict between the People and the Interests, it may nevertheless have involved a struggle by the middle class to preserve and further its moral and social values against threats from above and below.

Robert Wiebe's *Search for Order* contends that the central fact of the years from 1870 to 1920 was the erosion of small-town, autonomous, personal community life by forces that were nationalizing and urbanizing the economy and the polity. In the face of the chaos which these forces produced, he finds a number of responses: first, a fight on the part of the old middle class to preserve its informal social control of a homogeneous, familiar, stable society; then, an effort on the part of a vaguely defined elite called "men of power" to engage the help of the government in putting down the protests of the least privileged victims of this disorder; and finally, the emergence of a new middle class of specialists in business, labor, and agriculture which came to dominate American life with a confident commitment to professional administration of fluid social processes. This last is the response which Wiebe associates with progressivism. While I believe that Wiebe has located well the central dilemma of the period, and while I believe that he is correct that the style of the new middle class came not only to dominate the period but to stay, I also believe that his suggestion of an antithesis between this style and the goals either of the old middle class or of the business elite conceals some of the ironies of the period. It appears to me that the perception of the waning power of informal social control and the desire to find means of restoring it even in the context of urban industrialism contributed much of the moral indignation, energy, and even machinery which facilitated the rise of the professional managers. And it also appears that the interests of both the old and the new middle class in order and equilibrium did not interfere with the pursuit by a business elite of the climate in which to consolidate their economic and political power.

While the progressives themselves and some of their early chroniclers pictured the movement as both humanitarian and democratic, if the "lower orders" benefited by the progressive movement at all, it was by virtue of the efforts of others to moderate those excesses which might produce disruptive protest or which simply violated their own standards of decency. Progressivism was hardly a movement to redistribute power and wealth in fundamentally more equitable ways. In this and in other senses, progressivism may be called conservative.

It was also, however, innovative and aggressive in the devising of public, governmental machinery for the accomplishment of social ends. To some extent it simply consolidated, but to a large extent it also advanced the process of modernization. As Richard D. Brown has pointed out, the word "modern" has taken on a fixed, qualitative, as opposed to a relative, temporal meaning.[12] "Traditional" societies are composed of small communities, functionally undifferentiated, politically and economically self-sufficient, and dominated by a devotion to the past and a resignation to the future. "Modern" societies are built of large units, politically and economically integrated, each divided into functional specializations, considering change not only to be accepted but to be caused by rationalistic human manipulation. One must go centuries behind the progressive period to find Western society in a traditional state; the process of modernization, although proceeding unevenly along many fronts, appears a fairly continuous process across those centuries. But it seems to me to have crossed a crucial point in the United States in the late nineteenth and early twentieth centuries. In so long and continuous a process as modernization, all periods of time appear to be periods of transition, but the progressive movement seems to have brought the process to a new plateau of optimism concerning the capacity of people by bureaucratic and rationalistic means to control a nationally integrated collective experience.

The emergence of the juvenile court idea as a way of dealing with juvenile crime illustrates the step onto that plateau. The creation of the court marked the height of confidence in the possibility of reclaiming delinquents for an orderly and productive social life. Most of the ideas which made this confidence plausible have lost their force in the last three quarters of a century, and the consensus about the child and the state which produced the juvenile court movement has disintegrated. On the one hand are those who rage at the ineffectiveness of juvenile justice and wish to be tougher on young criminals. On the other are those who think the system as it is—particularly given its ineffectiveness—is quite tough enough and wish for a better way to protect delinquents from its workings. My interest is in how the juvenile court idea gained and lost the confidence of people concerned about delinquency. This focus puts the designers, defenders, and critics of the institution at the center and leaves aside the children and parents who pass through it: what follows is a history of ideas and institutions, not a social history.

I believe that the fate of this particular reform effort has implications which go beyond the matter of juvenile crime and its control. Just as the emergence of the juvenile court belonged to a larger process of modernization, the loss of faith in its effectiveness and fairness illustrates a more general disappointment with modern society, and particularly with spiraling aspirations toward progress by means of science and bureaucracy.

1

ORIGINS OF THE JUVENILE COURT

Wherever one dips into the history of the nineteenth century, one finds the fear that crime in general and juvenile crime in particular was on the rise in the cities. In 1823, James W. Gerard, a lawyer and member of the Society for the Prevention of Pauperism of New York, presented the society's report on the reformation of juvenile delinquents to a public meeting: he said that "it is with pain we state that, in five or six years past . . . the number of youth under fourteen years of age, charged with offenses against the law, has doubled."[1] In 1849, the police chief of the city of New York warned of the "constantly increasing numbers of vagrant, idle and vicious children of both sexes . . . who are growing up in ignorance and profligacy, only destined to a life of misery, shame and crime . . ."[2] Charles Loring Brace, founder of the New York Children's Aid Society, threatened in 1854 that the day might come when "the outcast, vicious, reckless multitude of New York boys, swarming now in every foul alley and low street, come to know their power and *use it.*"[3]

The era of the creation of the juvenile court is no exception. An article in the *Juvenile Record* of February 1902 about New York's new children's court reported:

> From many sources comes the suggestion that crime, among children, is rapidly increasing. . . . The magistrates, sitting

in various police courts for many years, are conscious that juvenile pickpockets, sneak thieves and burglars are rapidly increasing. Ten years ago such instances were extremely rare; today, in some sections of the city, they are extremely common.[4]

But while reports of mounting delinquency rates had considerable currency in the late nineteenth and early twentieth centuries and may have provided the impetus for reform, the talk among proponents of reform focused less on the dimensions of the problem than on the apparatus available for dealing with it.

That apparatus consisted of the criminal law, of course, and of institutions designed to house those found guilty of violating it. These were largely the legacy of a movement during and after the American Revolution to reform the criminal codes, and of a growing interest in the early nineteenth century in rehabilitating criminals through a process of reflection and penitence.

The efforts to revise the criminal codes took place under the influence of the "classical school" of criminology, which is associated particularly with the work of Cesare Beccaria and Jeremy Bentham in the late eighteenth and early nineteenth centuries. The classical school offered a system of justice which would curb the capricious exercise of judicial power and the use of the harshest punishments by matching the severity of the punishment to the severity of the crime. Such gradations might allow punishment to serve as deterrence and, where deterrence failed, set the stage for reformation of the criminal.

From the classical model derives a picture of the criminal as a free and responsible moral agent, at liberty to obey or disobey the law. The only factor which differentiated the criminal from the law-abiding citizen, and in that sense the only cause of crime, was the criminal's willingness to break the law.

[The classical school] assumed that men were endowed by nature with equal ability; that a man was a creature of free will who could choose to do right or wrong, and who should enjoy or suffer the consequences of his choice.[5]

If the only cause of crime was the choice to disobey, and if that cause was universal to all offenders, then the background of any criminal was irrelevant to the crime/punishment formula: if the *why* of criminality was already answered, the only matter that might properly concern the courts was *what* the individual had done. "The Classical School was not interested in the causes of crime."[6] The classical model logically implied a system of impartial and impersonal justice. The law need only express how repugnant a given crime was to society and apply a penalty that matched it in seriousness. The traditional rendering of justice as a blindfolded figure carrying scales is an apt symbol of the classical concept.

In the United States the classical formulation of the relationship between crime and punishment at first coexisted with the vestiges of a religious conviction that even minor offenses against the law were indications of fundamental moral depravity. In a predestinarian theology, with sinfulness located at the root of crime, there could be little hope of reforming the criminal and little inclination to examine what had led to his act. Investigations into the conditions of a criminal's life and speculations about the most effective treatment in any particular case promised no way out of what was assumed to be a permanent condition of social life.

David Rothman points out in *The Discovery of the Asylum* (Boston, 1971) that Jacksonian reformers shook themselves loose from doubts about reforming individual criminals and about reducing crime as a social phenomenon. They began to gather data about criminals, to construct biographies of them which pointed to the breakdown of family control and the existence of temptations in the environment rather than to sin as the source of crime. They turned their attention to the founding of "penitentiaries" that isolated inmates from each other and the world in the hope that solitude would provide time for contemplation, repentance, and redemption. They also created some special institutions for the reformation of young criminals. Houses of refuge in New York, Philadelphia, and Boston gathered in delinquent, dependent, and neglected children who by virtue of poverty and parental neglect needed residential care. In a combination of prison and school, apart from the world, they might learn through manual labor, religious and academic lessons the values of hard work and subordination. The Jacksonian reformers did not, however, alter the crime/punishment formula of the classical school; the regime of the penitentiaries and houses of refuge reflected by its inflexibility the conviction that there was essentially one cause of crime—moral failing—and one cure—a moral education.

Juvenile reformatories did not spread quickly in the early nineteenth century, but in the latter half of the century most states opened special institutions for children. These were usually modeled on the houses of refuge and their "congregate" organization of institutional life, in which "children of different ages and dispositions slept in cells or barracks-like dormitories [and] performed identical tasks according to a uniform schedule. . . ."[7] By the mid-nineteenth century, an alternative model of correctional institutions, based on family organization and called the cottage system, had captured the imagination of a new generation of reformers, and some had rejected institutionalization altogether in favor of "placing out" problem children with natural families, preferably farm families. But such experiments had little impact on the dominance of the Jacksonian model.

When the juvenile court was first conceived, the congregate reformatories offered the primary model for dealing with the problem of delinquency. They provided a correctional system which included notions of the distinctiveness of childhood and, thus, the necessity of segregating criminals by age. They were built upon the encouraging notion that, under strict supervision away from the normal world of excitement and temptation, children who broke the law could learn the values and habits which make upstanding citizens. The trouble with the system was that it failed.

By the late nineteenth century, the artificial environments

of the reformatories and even the institutions built on the cottage plan had earned reputations for both cruelty and ineffectiveness in rehabilitation. If they had ever been anything else, they had by then degenerated into custodial institutions which at best aided society by sparing it the company of criminals for a period of time, but which also served as a breeding ground for the attitudes which perpetuated crime. These institutions stood revealed not as agents of rehabilitation but as devices of punishment, and punishment had come to seem futile as a means of controlling crime. The colorful language of an article published in *The Arena* in 1893 expressed the futility of the punitive approach: "As well cut off an occasional thistle head with the expectation of killing the crop as to hope to exterminate crime through the deterrent power of penalty."[8] The statistics showed, it was thought, "that the majority of the criminal class are recidivists [and therefore] that our methods of everlastingly *punishing* have not in the case of the offender himself proved a deterrent."[9]

The problem with penal institutions and reformatories was not so much their harshness as their ineffectiveness. A study of delinquency published in 1908 explained:

> Mitigation of punishment as such is not the [new penology's] aim. The thing that adherents of this school are trying to do is substitute constructive efforts for the purely negative and destructive effects of the customary punishments. . . . The old system [of imprisonment] has proven itself to have one serious drawback—it doesn't work.[10]

If institutionalization equaled punishment and punishment equaled failure, something else was wanted for dealing with criminals.

A new school of criminology developed in the last quarter of the nineteenth century which offered both to explain the failure of incarceration and to point to methods which would be more constructive. This, the "positivist school" of criminology, challenged the notion that the singular cause of crime resided in the free moral choice of the criminal and consequently brought into question the idea that a uniform system of punishment based on the offense rather than the offender could either deter or rehabilitate.

Given the importance of environmentalism to the growth of the rehabilitative ideal, it is ironic that the nineteenth-century reaction against the model of the criminal as a free moral agent was fueled by the work of the Italian criminologist Cesare Lombroso, whose basic contribution was the idea that at least one class of criminals was born and not made. Although his resort to an explanation of crime as hereditary in origin temporarily diverted the rising tide of environmentalism, it nevertheless contributed to the emergence of an innovative approach to penology which could incorporate the environmentalist logic.

Lombroso began with the premise that whereas many crimes were committed by normal people overwhelmed by the passion or temptation of a passing moment, many others were committed by habitual criminals. Furthermore, the backgrounds of regular offenders, he claimed, often revealed no environmental explanation for their behavior. Since he rejected the notion of free will, and because he could not account for a large proportion of criminality by defects in environment and education, he sought the causes of crime in hereditary faults. He suggested that the habitual criminal was a case of atavism, or degeneracy, a throwback to the period in man's history when people had no laws and were willing to obey none. By observing the physical characteristics of criminals, he confirmed to his own satisfaction his belief that they were inherently different from law-abiding people. He concluded that the born criminal had clear physical stigmata that marked him from the occasional criminal and the normal person. Among the stigmata were asymmetry of the skull and face, scantiness or absence of beard, receding forehead, excessive length of face, dark hair and eyes, and tattooing. A person with five or more of these characteristics was a fully developed criminal.

Lombroso's theory was taken up, refined, and restated by Enrico Ferri in *Criminal Sociology*, published in 1884. Ferri, too, believed that there were two classes of criminals—the born and the occasional. Born criminals could be identified biologically but were a minority of the criminal population. Social and environmental conditions played a role in the genesis of both classes of criminals, since even if the disposition to crime was inherited by some, the form of crime was dictated by social setting.

Although Lombroso's physical definition of habitual criminality was soon discredited, he and his followers made a lasting contribution to criminology. First, by suggesting that at least some criminals acted not freely but under the constraint of forces beyond their control, they helped lift the burden of personal responsibility from the individual and to suggest, therefore, that punishment was senseless as a means of dealing with him. Second, by suggesting that there were several possible causes for crime, they focused attention on the offender as well as the offense. The positivist model demanded consideration of each criminal's background and personal traits as part of an intelligent disposition: it demanded a system of individualized justice in which punishment and deterrence were of limited relevance.

The view of the criminal as someone constrained or guided in his moral choices by forces beyond his control came to dominate the thinking of the period that produced the juvenile court: a book on child development published in 1898 explained the interaction of freedom and constraint for the ordinary person:

> . . . One is most apt to think of his freedom as permission to exercise himself within the demarcations set up by his environment; or one might compare it to the freedom which a prisoner, bound hand and foot, has to contract his muscles. In spite of such freedom he is still bound. And actually a member of a civilized community is bound physically, mentally and spiritually. He can no more be said to have real liberty of choice than a bird in a cage.[11]

This limitation on free moral choice was as true of the juvenile delinquent as it was of anyone else.

. . . Children, as a rule, act out in their lives the influences which have been brought to bear upon them. Their natural faculties are modifiable and are modified by their environment to such an extent that, in the main, responsibility for their careers is largely due to the influences in which they have spent the most plastic years of their life.[12]

Clarence Darrow, the famous reformer and "attorney for the damned," concluded in 1922:

All investigations have arrived at the results that crime is due to causes; that man is either not morally responsible or is responsible only to a slight degree. All have doubted the efficacy of punishment.[13]

The criminology of the late nineteenth century lightened the burden of moral responsibility for crime much as contemporary social thought lifted the blame for poverty from the shoulders of the poor.

The view of the criminal as constrained had attractive features. On the one hand, it appealed to an era fascinated with science. David Matza has pointed out:

. . . In the nineteenth as well as the early twentieth century, most intellectuals aspired to scientific status. . . . The advance of science required a recasting of man's nature. Notions of human reason and freedom were repugnant because they were the major basis for denying an easy equation of social with natural science.[14]

In order for man to be a valid subject of scientific inquiry, he too had to demonstrate like responses to like stimuli. A free will, which might at any time subvert the process of cause and effect, had no place in a scientific formulation of human behavior. On the other hand, the view of man as constrained appealed to the impulse to forgive and remold rather than condemn people for their failings.[15] A person who chose freely to disobey the law was contemptible; but a person compelled by forces beyond his control to disobey the law was an object for constructive sympathy and discipline, not condemnation. An article on criminality in children, written in 1899, expressed the hope that

> The time will come . . . when sin will be understood to mean misfortune; when moral defects will be treated like intellectual and physical defects: that is to say, as pathological cases, symptomatically, and not as punishable crimes.[16]

Under the influence of Lombroso and his followers, late-nineteenth-century reformers concerned with delinquency became committed to the view of the criminal as constrained, but they rejected Lombroso's concentration on physical stigmata and heredity. Although professional criminologists may have turned from biological to environmental positivism later than reformers, their literature in the 1890's tended at least to mix environmental considerations into evolutionary analyses.

While hereditarian explanations did not disappear altogether, the environmental facts of industrialization and urbanization dominated the explanations of crime put forward during the early juvenile court movement. The industrial city had many evils: its pace of life made parents too busy and too insensitive to supervise their children properly; its lavishness excited cupidity; in its crowds, the activities of criminals went unnoticed and potential criminals were emboldened by seeing that crime could pay; its economy drew children too early into the labor force, where they met adults of questionable character and where they found too much freedom. The city intensified the struggle for existence: the weakest were left by the wayside to grow bitter and antisocial, and others developed a mood of suspicion and distrust. The criminologist William Douglas Morrison wrote in 1897:

> These conditions of existence are destructive of social cohesion in its highest forms, and have the tendency to develop the selfish instincts till they overstep the border-land which separates selfishness from crime.[17]

The real culprit, however, was not the city itself: it was poverty in the urban setting. The urban disorder described by environmental positivists rarely marred the experience of the urban rich, but it was the daily fare of the poor. In its simplest form, this economic determinism maintained that poor people stole to get what they could not otherwise have. In the 1890's and 1900's the Proceedings of the National Conference of Charities and Correction and such magazines as *The Charities and the Commons* were filled with suggestions of a one-to-one relationship between economic deprivation and antisocial behavior. Or, if the relationship was not quite so direct, there was an easy progression from poverty to physical and moral decay to crime.

Bad nutrition, poor hearing and eyesight, and adenoidal growths—not serious problems unless they went untended, as they did in the slums—eroded the child's powers of concentration, made him a failure at school, and drove him in desperation to the streets, where temptation awaited him. The physical weakness that resulted from poverty haunted the slum dweller all his life, preventing him from competing in the labor market, condemning him to a life of economic hopelessness, and ultimately crime.

The moral side effects of poverty were even more serious than the physical. Whether because of drunkenness and vice, or because of the constant struggle to keep a family clothed and fed, or because they were themselves new to America and disoriented, slum parents did not give their children sufficient social and moral training. Through overexposure, even upstanding slum parents became hardened and accustomed to immoral and criminal people around them and failed to combat their influence on the children. Since children learned primarily through imitation, their futures depended on the examples they found in their environment.

Thus, the environmentalist wing of the "positivist" school of criminology put the burden of responsibility on society: economic and social systems produced citizens who were physically and morally unfit for social life, and adults ill equipped or disinclined to raise children properly. Edward

Devine, pioneer social worker and once a president of the National Conference of Charities and Correction, clearly blamed the social context for individual malfunction.

> One may understand crime and the criminal precisely in the degree in which he comprehends that it is not the individual standing there at whom stones are to be thrown, but literally the community itself, the individuals who surround the prisoner—judge, jury, advocate, and spectators—above all the spectators—are responsible for this thing that we call crime.[18]

But if the social context, rather than individual and fundamental depravity, was responsible, something could be done. People were born with the potential to assume various roles; what became of them depended on the conditions into which they were born and in which they were raised. Where others had seen individual human failings as the cause of social disarray, progressives attempted to reverse the causal chain: social ills now constituted the cause rather than the result of defective character. The evolution of the species, carried out though it was by the mechanism of biological heredity, was itself a response to values dictated by environmental conditions. By manipulating the environment in which people lived, reformers believed that they could call forth the qualities which permitted humane and orderly social life and discourage those qualities which disrupted it. The long-term painstaking approaches of spiritual or genetic purification could be brushed aside for the immediate satisfactions of slum clearance, temperance legislation, and settlement houses. The process could begin at once with generations already born, and need in theory surrender only the rare few to the ranks of the hopeless. Environmentalism was a source of optimism for reformers interested in corrections, as it was for other progressive reformers. Although the penitentiary had made little headway against crime, society should not abandon its efforts to combat crime. On the contrary, it should redouble them. But the effort must take the form of attention to the causes of crime in particular cases and of cures which responded to the nature of the offender, not to the nature of the offense.

The juvenile court reformers shared this faith in the possibility of redirecting the lives of other human beings. And if the late nineteenth century seemed, with the reformulation of the rehabilitative ideal, an auspicious time for the convicted adult criminal, it was more auspicious for the young offender. A burgeoning child-study movement, with its beginnings in the 1870's, illustrated growing interest in and sympathy for the child. In the 1890's, such new magazines as *Pedagogical Seminary, Child Study Monthly, Child Life,* and *Children's Charities* carried on discussions about the dynamics and problems of child development. By 1895, a number of universities had initiated child-study programs. In the progressive period the child was one intended beneficiary, if not the only one, of campaigns to end the use of child labor and extend the scope of compulsory education. Robert Wiebe writes: "If humanitarian progressivism had a central theme, it was the child. He united the campaigns for health, education, and a richer city environment, and he dominated much of the interest in labor legislation."[19] He also generated special concern among criminologists and penal reformers.

Given the assumption that man is amenable to improvement by the conscious application of modifying forces, the fascination of nineteenth-century social thinkers with children is understandable. Theologians and reformers in the Jacksonian period engaged in a great debate about the nature and nurture of the child, but by the end of the century, the quality and quantity of emotional and intellectual investment in children had changed. Bernard Wishy's *The Child and the Republic,* published in 1968, expresses the change in the titles of its two main sections: "The Child Redeemable (1830–1860)" and "The Child Redeemer (1860–1900)." Influenced by evolutionary thought to consider consciously the direction and nature of progress, anxious about the future of America as they had known it, hopeful about the capacity of expertise to deal with social issues, and convinced that the happy future of mankind depended on the conservation of resources, the progressives turned a scientific child-study movement to conserve human resources in the most economical way, by beginning when human beings were most plastic, when they were children.

A friend of Ralph Waldo Emerson's lamented the transformation in nineteenth-century attitudes to children by saying: "It was a misfortune to have been born when children were nothing, and to live till men were nothing." This shift of interest achieved fuller institutionalized and theoretical expression in the late nineteenth century. Moving from the cautious optimism of the early decades of the century, which allowed that child nature contained sufficient potential for good to be tapped by careful training, the theory of child nurture which characterized the last decades gave considerably more latitude to the natural qualities of children and demonstrated significantly more faith in their goodness. What Tocqueville had noticed in family relationships in the Jacksonian era as greater equality, intimacy, and spontaneity between parent and child in a democratic society, had by the end of the century found theoretical expression in writers who emphasized the natural exuberance of children, urged parents to accept and forgive it, and warned them to respect the boundaries between their own world of duties and responsibilities and the world of their children, which should rightfully be one of pleasure and freedom.

The view of the child put forward in the child-study literature of the late nineteenth century (and shared by founders of the juvenile court) centered on the notion of the child's innocence. Innocence in this context had at least two meanings: one suggested a lack of responsibility for a particular act or event; another suggested an enduring purity and freedom from vice. These concepts of innocence summarized two related but divergent factions of the child-study movement.

The more clinical and hardheaded side of the movement believed in the child's innocence in the first sense: it acknowledged faults of childhood, faults which in adults would be inexcusable, but insisted that they represented an involuntary and necessary part of child development. This faction pictured the child as a little savage. Alexander Chamberlain's *The Child, a Study in the Evolution of Man*, written in 1901, exemplifies this thinking. By extending the idea that ontogeny recapitulates phylogeny to postnatal character development, these writers concluded that man after birth was destined to reenact in microcosm the history of the species.

> This view [Chamberlain wrote] that the individual more or less distinctly repeats at least the chief stages in the development of the race, both mentally and physically, has been accepted as the cardinal doctrine of the newer theories of education.[20]

Henry King Lewis expressed the same view in *The Child, Its Spiritual Nature* in 1896:

> The first year of a child's life may represent the full-grown prehistoric man. The gradual development of the infant mind, year by year, supplies an epitome of the race.[21]

Childhood was merely a repetition of the savage stage in man's history.

The keynote of the savage stage had been its amorality: the savage had ministered to his own needs regardless of the effect on other people; he had known no social law and recognized no right of property (save perhaps his own). Thus, it should have shocked no one that the child-as-savage was amoral and indifferent to the laws of society. Nor should it have caused anyone to despair, for if the infant were destined by natural developments to be amoral, the adolescent was destined by the same processes to develop religious and altruistic motives, just as the race had developed them. In the end, the moral and law-abiding condition was to be as natural to normal adults as the amoral and law-defying state had been to the normal child. The development of respect for accepted morality became a built-in feature of man, and his temporary stage of amorality had to be excused.

Such an understanding of innocence—the child seen as not responsible by virtue of biological necessity—was in counter-

point to the more sentimental faction of the child-study movement, whose image of the child as the essence of goodness and
the absence of guile corresponded to the second definition of
innocence: moral purity in its first moment of existence. This
perspective on childhood, appearing side by side with the first
in the issues of *Pedagogical Seminary* and other such journals,
held that the faults of children were due to ignorance of
specific social rules, but that such ignorance was easily overcome since the child had an innate willingness to submit to
authority. Moreover, the great principles of right and wrong
belonged at birth to the child. A study called *The Psychology
of Childhood* revealed in 1909:

> Moral ideas do not require to be created or implanted in the
> minds of children by their elders. Nothing is more certain
> than that the child is born potentially a moral being, possess-
> ing a moral nature which requires only to be evoked and de-
> veloped by environmental conditions.[22]

Innate religious instincts were also attributed to children by
no less a student of child development than G. Stanley
Hall.[23] If this innate moral sense was not destroyed by early
experience, and was cultivated by the child's elders, it would
carry him naturally into a state of moral adulthood. This view
of the child as innately moral enjoyed substantial popularity
during the late nineteenth century and was shared by Judge
Benjamin Lindsey, one of the most influential leaders of the
juvenile court movement.[24]

Although there was disagreement within the child-study
movement about the stage at which moral character developed
in children, there was a very important core of concurrence:
first, both sides agreed that the normal adult abided by moral
and social rules; and second, they agreed that if normal children did not, their antisocial behavior was not the fault of the
children themselves. Such a view of childhood implied a constructive, nonpunitive approach to juvenile misbehavior which
concentrated on providing a healthy, respectable family environment which would not interfere with and might guide
the natural unfolding of a moral adult.

Developments in criminology and in child study reinforced each other and combined to encourage reforms in juvenile justice. Both produced ideas which reduced the child offender's burden of moral responsibility; both shifted the emphasis from punishment and severity to constructive and flexible treatment. In the late nineteenth century there was some experimentation with correctional tools that would introduce flexibility to the treatment of adult criminals: support grew for the indeterminate sentence, parole, probation, and noninstitutional treatment as alternatives to fixed sentences in prisons with rigid regimes. In view of the growing interest in and tolerance for the differences between children and adults, it is not surprising that such efforts should reach their fullest expression in the treatment of juvenile offenders. And in view of the evolving philosophy of the responsible state, it was possible for reformers to turn to government to mediate between the child and a destructive environment.

The final ingredient, the catalyst which the reformers themselves tell us extracted a plan of action from a state of mind, was their indignation at the inhumane treatment of children in criminal law and the barbarity of the conditions under which child criminals were confined. The experience of reformers in Illinois, where the first juvenile court law passed in 1899, is illustrative. In spite of promises which had surrounded the reform-school system, by 1885 the state had no reformatory for delinquent girls and "the boys' reformatory was essentially a miniature prison, based on the stern principle of retribution for offenses committed against the criminal law."[25] There was much public criticism of the state's institutional treatment of child offenders during the 1870's and eighties, most notably by the State Board of Public Charities, which focused on overcrowding and the absence of constructive programs. Lucy Flower, a major figure in the juvenile court movement, attributed the movement's beginnings in Illinois to the inspection of state institutions by her friend and colleague Julia Lathrop. Miss Lathrop was appointed to the State Board of Public Charities by Governor John Peter Altgeld. Flower recalled that "up to that time, visitation of

state and county institutions had been largely perfunctory.
. . . Miss Lathrop . . . went to every jail and poorhouse
in the state. . . . She was shocked at the conditions she
found, young children shut up with the most depraved adults
and being trained in crime, instead of being kept away from
it."[26] Efforts to improve the conditions of institutional life—
among these the creation of a jail school by the Chicago
Women's Club in 1890—met with little success. Frustrated
with this approach, Mrs. Flower's Everyday Club allied with
the State Board of Public Charities and other child-saving
groups to explore new ideas, particularly that of a special court
for children. Similar frustration with efforts to reform institutional conditions prodded child savers elsewhere.

The reformers also expressed dissatisfaction with the
criminal law for failing to distinguish between young
offenders and adults, as if they were moral and psychological
equals. They objected to a system of criminal justice and a
courtroom procedure which paid no attention to the offender
but only to the offense. What the reformers tell us, however,
about the outrageous judicial dispositions of juvenile cases
before the creation of the juvenile court is evidently closer to
the system as it existed on paper than to its operation in
reality. There is evidence, occasionally in the testimony of the
reformers themselves, that before the legislative creation of
juvenile courts judges in many jurisdictions were trying to
bend the classical system to accommodate the child offender
better. Judges frequently reduced or suspended sentences for
children or let them go entirely, rather than send them to jail.
Reformers sometimes persuaded judges to hold separate hearings for children and to permit the participation of volunteer
probation officers. In many cases of alleged brutality to children in the name of the criminal law, the "victims" never
actually suffered the punishment prescribed by law.[27]

But to say that the situation for child offenders in criminal
court was more lenient in reality than it might have been is
not to undercut entirely the reformers' claim to humanitarian
impulses. Prisons and jails must indeed have been grim places
for children to share with adult criminals. The reformatories

were evidently not much better, even if they did do some honor to the principle of age segregation. Furthermore, if one believed that a judicial and penal system should differentiate on the basis of age, why should one be content with the *ad hoc* measures that sometimes kept children out of criminal courts; why should one depend on the good will of each particular judge when the principles might be inscribed in the law for all to follow? But most important for these reformers, benevolent supervision, not leniency, gave meaning to humanitarian reform. Their dissatisfaction was with a system that seemed to offer the choice of a guilty verdict—which might subject the child to adult penalties—or a not-guilty verdict or a suspended sentence—which would subject him neither to penalties nor to constructive control. They were frankly in search of a system which would make the law and the courts more effective agencies in the lives of young offenders, not a means to exempt them from the law altogether. They believed that the criminal law and the facilities available to house its convicts could not, in part because of their punitive and inflexible natures, meet the need. The goal was the protection and improvement of society: nonpunitive, preferably noninstitutional, educational methods offered a more potent means to that goal. The reformers were fortunate to have a cause which seemed to them to serve the children by greater kindness and understanding at the same time that it served the public by greater effectiveness in controlling crime.

Unfortunately, it is typical of the life cycle of reform that the fusion of social control with greater humaneness is a tenuous one which typically dissolves, leaving the machinery for social control firmly entrenched—even if it is ineffective—after the spirit of humanitarianism has departed. Such was the fate of the Jacksonian machinery for the rehabilitation of criminals, the penitentiary, which was adopted during the course of the nineteenth century with such high hopes. Such may now appear to be the fate of the juvenile court. The failure of these efforts, given the historical odds, may throw reformism itself into question, but it is not proof that the element of authoritarianism was from the first the essence of the movement. At any rate, there was no contradiction in the minds of juvenile court reformers between the twin goals of justice and compassion, and they thought they could build an institution which would serve both goals better than they had ever been served before.

2
THE IDEAL
JUVENILE COURT

The juvenile court movement emerged from frustration with the dominant modes of dealing with child offenders. But the willingness to dispense with the old did not itself give form to the new. Those who condemned the old system as harsh and ill conceived had still to define a specific program, both more humane and more effective than the criminal law and the penal system. As general principles, the founders of the juvenile court adopted the tenets of contemporary child study and positivist criminology. As the nearest approximation of a concrete model in harmony with those principles, they had the example of the state of Massachusetts.

Beginning in 1869, Massachusetts law had provided for the participation of visiting agents or officers of the State Board of Charities in juvenile cases: these agents investigated juvenile cases and made recommendations to the judges for disposition. Between 1870 and 1877, a series of measures established separate hearings, dockets, and records for children under sixteen, and a program of visitation by probation officers to homes in which delinquent children had been "placed out." With separate hearings for children and a rudimentary probation system, Massachusetts had gone further than any other state in modifying criminal procedure and criminal sanctions in children's cases. It had not gone far enough, but it provided an example on which to build a system which would relieve child offenders of the undeserved burden of criminal responsibility and yet prevent them from going astray again.

Perhaps the most influential idea in shaping the juvenile court system was the thesis that the defect which produced juvenile crime lay not so much in the child as in the environment from which he had come and, therefore, that no child should be treated as a criminal. The child, naturally or at least potentially innocent and moral, learned antisocial behavior from contact with corrupt adults. Accordingly, the first principle of the new court apparatus and its ancillary institutions was to separate the child from adult offenders at all times. The notion that child saving depended on separation of children from adults was not new to the progressive period: the house of refuge had been organized on the same principle in the early nineteenth century. But the persisting incarceration of juveniles with adults in detention and correctional facilities and their commingling in the courtroom led progressive reformers to carry to its logical conclusion the effort to disentangle juvenile justice from adult justice. In this cause, juvenile court legislation usually prohibited the confinement of children with adults, and occasionally made nonsegregated confinement itself punishable as a misdemeanor. In the literature and the laws, founders of the juvenile court demanded not only separate reformatories but separate detention centers, and separate sessions or courtrooms as well.

Mandatory age segregation made implicitly the accusation that adult criminals were one cause of childhood corruption. Noncriminal adults also had to share the responsibility. In 1903, the Colorado legislature passed the first state law holding parents and guardians legally responsible for contributing to the delinquencies of their children.[1] Judge Ben Lindsey, pioneer of the Denver juvenile court and leader among reformers and defenders of wayward youth, claimed that the contributing-to-delinquency law "has done more than anything else to solve the problems of delinquency with us."[2] He considered the fining and jailing of citizens who encouraged or permitted delinquency in children under their charge his state's greatest contribution to the movement. Many localities followed Denver in coupling their juvenile court laws with provisions giving the court jurisdiction over contributing adults. These provisions gave institutional expression to the theory that the child was not ultimately responsible for his acts.

The reformers sought further expression of that theory and further detachment from the criminal law by trying to dispel from juvenile court proceedings the atmosphere of blame and recrimination which they detected in criminal proceedings. They hoped to remove entirely from the juvenile court process the implication that the child was capable of criminal intent or subject to criminal sanctions. In this they began at the beginning—with the mode of initiating cases. Ideally, initiation by petition was to replace initiation by complaint. By this process any reputable person might bring to the attention of the court a child he had reason to believe delinquent within the meaning of the law or in need of the court's supervision. Unlike the complainant, the petitioner need have had no direct connection with the case, and was presumably engaged in securing help for the child rather than seeking revenge. The reformers hoped that this change would bring more needy and troublesome children into court, and make apparent to such children that the court took action out of interest in their welfare and not out of anger. Behind this change in procedure one senses an image of community involvement with the welfare of children that bears greater resemblance to disappearing village life than to the urban disorder with which the juvenile court was supposed to cope. But whether the right of petition was placed in the public at large or only in a probation staff which would screen referrals, the process was in contrast to criminal procedure in its emphasis on sympathetic rather than accusatory initiations. A similar purpose animated the recommended shift from a warrant for arrest to a summons as the court's means of compelling the appearance of a child who had been brought to its attention.

To realize the constructive potential of court control, the founders recommended that at some time between petition and hearing an officer of the court conduct a preliminary investigation into the background of the child. The officer's mission was to unearth information which might point to the source of the child's misbehavior and suggest the proper remedy. While in a criminal case the preparation for trial would focus upon evidence concerning the commission of a specific prohibited act, here the preparation for a hearing was to give full scope to a systematic and sympathetic inquiry which could form the basis for a disposition based on the circumstances of the child's life rather than on the question of guilt or innocence. The reformers hoped to effectuate as well as to symbolize the fusion of the interests of the child with those of society by placing responsibility for this investigation in the hands of the probation officer, who was by law required to represent the child, and at the same time to serve the court. The functions of defense counsel and prosecuting attorney, so far as they remained, now fell to a single individual.

That person also assumed responsibility for the accused during the detention period. In contrast to criminal proceedings, where the right to bail might postpone the impact of the state upon the accused until guilt had been proven beyond a reasonable doubt, juvenile court proceedings included the option of a constructive detention period that could serve as the opening stage of a reformation process for children whose hearings had not even commenced. Before the child appeared in court he might be separated from his parents and placed in the charge of a probation officer or in a detention home, not because he was otherwise unlikely to appear at his hearing, but because the reformers presumed that he would benefit by state supervision whether he proved to be delinquent or not, and because the detention period would allow the gathering of important data for the hearing.

In order that every stage of the child's experience with the court contribute to the reformation of his character, the founders set to work to modify courtroom procedure as well. They intended to sweep away all elements of criminal trials "so that an intimate, friendly relationship [might] be established at once between the judge and the child."[3] The reformers so favored procedural informality that they made it a crucial test of the adequacy of a juvenile court system. They insisted that the true juvenile court could not be criminal at all, that its proceedings had to be civil in fact as well as in form. While a few reformers in some states thought it wise to allow for jury trials and defense counsel on demand, they did so "in order to avoid constitutional difficulties or attacks upon the law" and not because they believed that "any such provisions are necessary."[4] Generally, juvenile court reformers regarded juries and lawyers as unnecessary restraints upon the flexible pursuit of the best interests of the child.

The elimination of procedural formality in the courtroom presumably freed the judge to employ all available resources in gaining the child's confidence and thereby beginning the resocialization process. In this context, the kind of person who served as juvenile court judge became extemely important. Participants in the movement frequently stated their conviction that the success of the juvenile court turned upon the capability of the judge.

Juvenile court literature exhibited relatively little concern with the qualities usually associated with a judge—a thorough knowledge of the law, an independent and even-handed sense of justice. Rather, it asserted the desirability of a judge who would appeal personally to the youngsters brought before him. Judge Ben Lindsey believed that "more is accomplished through love than by any other method,"[5] and most of the court's supporters agreed that the emphasis belonged on sympathy rather than on legal learning. In the juvenile court movement, Lindsey's own brand of friendly and fatherly involvement in the lives of delinquent children served as a model for the approach which Stephen Schlossman has called "affectional discipline."[6] The emphasis on personal qualities of wisdom and kindness did not, however, imply that the juvenile court judge might be an amateur at his duties: the reformers conceived of the juvenile court judgeship as a full-time specialty demanding the exclusive and long-term attention of the person who filled it.

The judge's task was, of course, to weigh all available evidence of the child's circumstances and to prescribe a treat-

ment if treatment were in order. In collecting data about the
child, the judge could and should allow testimony of any sort,
irrespective of such constraints from criminal procedure as the
rule against hearsay evidence. No scruples about the legal
appropriateness of testimony in a criminal court could have
outweighed in the founders' minds the potential value of
knowing everything there was to know about the child and his
environment.

The reformers overhauled court procedure in an effort,
they said, to minimize future negative repercussions in the life
of the offender. In order to prevent society from unjustly
stigmatizing children who had appeared in court the reformers recommended the exclusion of all persons from juvenile
court hearings except those directly involved in the case. The
constitutional guarantee of a public trial seemed to them to
carry more danger than protection. As a further precaution,
the architects of the court suggested that only officials have
access to the records of juvenile court proceedings and that
evidence gathered in connection with such cases be inadmissi-
ble in any other court. Finally, the reformers recommended
that juvenile courts make general adjudications of delinquency rather than of specific offenses, also in the hope that
such general adjudications would be less stigmatizing.

Once having found the child delinquent, the court still had
before it the most important part of its job—the formulation
of an intelligent course of treatment, which meant by definition a course that took its direction from the specific needs of
the child in question. Punishment to fit the crime might be
uniform, but treatment to fit the child had to be individualized, and treatment rather than punishment was the business of
the juvenile court. In 1884, John Peter Altgeld made a classic
statement of the medical analogy which persuaded so many
reformers of the appropriateness of individualized justice:

> If the state were to enforce a system of medical practice and
> were to provide that but one prescription should be given for
> all the ills that afflict the flesh, it would not be more absurd
> than is the present system of treating offenders.[7]

In 1926, the director of the Psychopathic Clinic in Detroit expressed the continuing scorn of juvenile court supporters for the notion that a "uniform system of treating all crime is going to be any more successful than a uniform system of treating all fevers would be."[8]

In pursuit of the ideal of individualized treatment, the reformers seemed to imagine an infinite range of choice in tailoring the disposition to fit the child. Nevertheless, both practical considerations and the premises of the movement itself circumscribed the judge's choice.

One of the distinctive features of the juvenile court movement was its primary, if not exclusive, commitment to probation as the most desirable disposition for child offenders. Where other generations had channeled their dissatisfaction with correctional institutions into redesigning such institutions, the progressives concentrated on developing an alternative which could occupy the foreground of juvenile corrections while the last resort (or threat) of institutionalization remained in the background. With the exception of a diagnostic detention period, a cardinal rule of the juvenile court movement and of child-welfare work in general in this period was that whenever possible the child should receive what care he needed in a home—either his own or some other—rather than in an institution.

The preference for home rehabilitation still left the judge the choice of returning the child to his own home under the supervision of a probation officer or of having him placed in a new one. In this choice the reformers, and frequently the laws, guided the judge to make the first effort with the parents and to place a child in a foster home only if necessary. If the child was to be placed with another family, it was desirable that the relationship as closely as possible approximate a natural family setting. But except for the differences inherent in institutional and home living, the location and duration of the child's treatment were the only variables with which the courts could work directly. Whatever manipulation of the child's environment was actually to take place was likely to fall to the judgment and skill of the probation officer.

Regardless of the disposition of particular cases, the reformers intended that the child's experience with the court be free of accusation and full of constructive and friendly discipline. In all its dealings with delinquent children, the court was to take as its model the protective attitude of the state toward children who were abandoned or neglected or abused by their parents or guardians. A finding of delinquency might focus on the behavior of the child, while a finding of dependency or neglect focused on the behavior of his parents, but the former was only a symptom of the latter. The distinctions between dependent, neglected, and delinquent children were less important than their common need for state supervision in the manner of a wise and devoted parent. To each other and to the public the reformers pictured the court as a clinic for moral ills, an agent of moral and intellectual improvement, a school for the offending child and for the community. They proudly agreed that the juvenile court embodied a new understanding of the problem of delinquency and a new ideal of the relationship between society and its lawbreakers. Looking back over the first twenty years of the juvenile court movement, the executive secretary of the Ohio Humane Society wrote in 1922: "Against the old herd instinct we have a newer and more altruistic impulse, in which all society gets together in an effort of reclamation."[9]

The reformers continually made these aims explicit and constantly put them in the foreground of their literature. But the tone of juvenile court propaganda and the implications of juvenile court techniques suggest that the goals of the reformers and the significance of the movement did not fit solely under the heading of more humane and effective treatment for child offenders. Or rather, the heading is too vague to convey fully the assumptions of the juvenile court movement or to reveal how its assumptions have made it vulnerable to criticism in spite of the general appeal of its stated goals.

The juvenile court promised the community that it would purge delinquents of their antisocial tendencies by giving them specialized treatment. The reformers pursued the ideal of such treatment by collecting data on the child's home life, school record, physical health, economic status, and so on. This aspect of the evidence, which reformers called "social" testimony, became so important to court supporters that they allowed and even encouraged it to overshadow evidence bearing upon questions of "guilt" or "innocence"—words which they rarely permitted to pass their lips. This studied disinterest in the facts of the alleged act of delinquency was often explicit. Julian Mack, the second judge of the Chicago juvenile court and an active participant in the movement, addressed an American Bar Association audience in 1909:

> The problem for determination by the [juvenile court] judge is not, has this boy or girl committed a specific wrong, but what is he, how has he become what he is. . . .[10]

A survey of juvenile courts published in 1920 found:

> . . . The fundamental purpose of juvenile court proceedings is not to determine whether or not a child has committed a specific offense, but to discover whether he is in a condition requiring the special care of the State. . . .[11]

While the literature customarily justified disinterest in specific offenses by a higher interest in providing children with needed guidance, and while this disinterest was in a way consistent with the movement's stated aim of benefiting the child, it suggested another aim as well. It suggested that the founders and supporters of the juvenile court were not exclusively or perhaps even primarily interested in juvenile offenders as that term had been understood before the passage of juvenile court laws but in a far broader area of jurisdiction, both over the child and over his family.

For the most part, before 1899, a child offender was a person who had broken a law or ordinance and who also happened to be a minor: his age, not his act, differentiated him from the adult offender. However, by minimizing questions of guilt and innocence of specific criminal acts, the founders changed the focus of correctional efforts. Far from simply trying to secure better treatment for children who had been con-

victed of illegal acts, they were directing their efforts to a
newly defined and greatly enlarged class of children—those
who seemed to need the state's care whether or not they had
in a strict sense committed an offense, and who might never
have otherwise come within the reach of the law. While un-
dertaking to extend to child criminals the protection which
had previously been afforded neglected or dependent children, the juvenile court reformers were also casting a net that
could catch children who might hitherto have eluded legal
sanction: children who were neither dependent nor neglected
nor guilty of a criminal offense. A manual for probation
officers in New York State explained the virtues of unofficial
probation for children who had not so much as appeared in
court by pointing out:

> In many cases the delinquency is so incipient or the family
> circumstances are such that unless the cases could be dealt
> with unofficially they would never come to the attention of
> the court, or if they should, not until it was too late to secure
> the results possible through early unofficial treatment.[12]

The ideal juvenile court and probation system was to be
available for rehabilitative work with children even where
official court action was unwarranted.

The definition of delinquency which eventually prevailed
in juvenile court laws illustrated more graphically the reformers' desire to reach beyond juvenile criminals to influence the
lives of other "unfortunate" children. Only a few juvenile
court statutes stopped at the boundaries of old definitions—
with children who had violated laws or ordinances. Reformers
criticized such statutes, including the original Illinois law, and
sought to amend them. They much preferred laws that included such offenses as smoking cigarettes, fighting, using
profane language, habitually walking along railroad tracks,
frequenting houses of prostitution, associating with thieves,
running away from home, growing up in idleness, idly wan-
dering the streets at night, or being "incorrigible." Grace
Abbott's 1910 abstract of juvenile court laws declared:

Better laws make the definition much more inclusive so that the court will not be unable, because of any technical lack of jurisdiction, to place a child under the care of the court . . . if that seems to be for the best interest of the child.[13]

It is true that before the passage of juvenile court laws techniques were available to reach children who did some of the things which were now named as noncriminal conduct warranting a finding of delinquency. In some states "incorrigibility" had been grounds for commitment to a house of refuge, and disorderly-conduct laws undoubtedly brought to the criminal courts children who committed no independently criminal offense. Julia Lathrop described the juvenile clientele of the Chicago police courts just before the Illinois juvenile court act came into effect:

> 332 boys between the ages of nine and sixteen years were sent to the city prison. Three hundred and twenty of them were sent up on the blanket charge of disorderly conduct, which covered offenses from burglary and assault with a deadly weapon to picking up coal on the railway tracks, building bonfires, playing ball in the street, or "flipping trains," that is, jumping on and off moving cars. . . . Out of the 332 cases sent to the Bridewell during the first half of the year 1899, nearly one-third were pardoned by the mayor.[14]

This was the dilemma which provoked juvenile court reformers: the criminal law gave the alternatives of commitment to correctional institutions which had proven cruel failures, or of pardon (or acquittal) to avoid commitment. While the reformers undoubtedly wished through probation to avoid incarceration, they also wished to avoid the alternative of nonintervention. The lengthening list of noncriminal acts which warranted a finding of delinquency was intended to bring within the purview of the juvenile court the many children who were " 'let off' by the justice or pardoned by the mayor" and on whose behalf, consequently, "no constructive work was done."[15]

By blurring the distinctions between dependent, neglected,

and delinquent children, by minimizing questions of guilt or innocence of specific acts, and by including in the definition of delinquency noncriminal conduct, the juvenile court reformers were intentionally advocating a jurisdiction for the court which would augment the power of the state to intervene in the lives of children and in the relationships between the children and their parents.

Some scholars, Anthony Platt most notable among them, have implied that this expansiveness in the definition of delinquency gives the lie to the humanitarian claims of the juvenile court movement.[16] There is much to learn from this and other signs of the reformers' desire to expand state intervention into the lives of children and their families, but it is not direct evidence on the question of how "humane" were the intentions of juvenile court reformers. The usefulness of the question is mitigated by the danger that we are using more than one meaning of "humanitarian." First, the expansive definition of delinquency may have been largely intended to bring within the jurisdiction of the juvenile court acts which otherwise would have been gathered into the criminal courts under the label of disorderly conduct, as they were in Chicago just before the juvenile court law took effect. It is worth noting that the same behavior in juvenile court might bring years of probation until the age of majority was reached, while they might be followed by no action at all in criminal court or by sentences quite limited in time. But unless the definition of "humane" is irrevocably linked to nonintervention, even this observation does not give the lie to the reformers. Their definition of humanitarian treatment of children certainly was not mere leniency or nonintervention: it was constructive discipline, and this is not or was not an altogether implausible definition, even if it has little appeal in the present.

If the reformers had been accused of overextending juvenile court jurisdiction, they might have countered that such expansion of state intervention would prevent crime by bringing children within the scope of the law before their delinquent tendencies became criminal. And, indeed, prevention of crime counted among the founders' avowed intentions. Stephen Schlossman finds this aspect one of the few that really distinguish the ideas of the juvenile court movement from reform efforts on behalf of child offenders in the early nineteenth century.[17]

The defense of extended jurisdiction as a preventive measure against crime would have constituted an interesting though somewhat elliptical claim, since it omitted the vital demonstration of what represented a symptom of future criminality. The literature lacked any tightly reasoned argument to the effect that the commission of one of the new offenses indicated a propensity for the commission of genuine crimes later in life or to the effect that, in specific terms, boys who wandered around railroad tracks or used profane language were more likely than most eventually to rob banks. Nor was there any serious effort in the literature to make the more indirect connection between such behavior and laxness of parental control, which was in turn regarded as the breeding ground of more serious offenses. The issue of what constituted proto-criminal behavior was either too complicated or too self-evident to discuss. Or perhaps the relative silence on the subject reveals that the reformers were as dedicated to controlling these acts as an end in itself as they were to using them to detect potential criminals. While ostensibly legislating on matters of crime and punishment, they also legislated their preferences in the realm of manners and morals. By allowing noncriminal behavior on the part of children to trigger the intervention of a probation officer into family life, the juvenile court reformers were placing their movement among a number of others which were, in the progressive period, sending numerous missionaries from the dominant culture to the lower classes to acculturate immigrants, to teach mothers household management, and to supervise the recipients of charity.

Occasionally, the notions of individualized justice and positivist criminology were frankly linked by their advocates to the aim of stricter social control. But on a less explicit and philosophical plane, there were many indications that juvenile

court supporters intended more than the mere control of criminal behavior in children and more even than the prevention
of criminal behavior in future adults. Judge Lindsey wanted
not only "to teach children how and why they should obey the
law" but also to make the children "really patriotic in spirit,
protectors of the state and upholders of its laws."[18] Others
hoped to direct the delinquent's thoughts into "pure channels
and higher ideals for virtue and pure manhood," and to teach
an "appreciation of the true, the beautiful, and the good,"
"neatness, cleanliness and correctness, and . . . a love and
respect for other people's property and opinions."[19] Such
statements elevated the mores of the middle class to the level
of universal values, but even if these mores had been universally shared, they were not the usual business of a court of
law, and went well beyond the stated aim of discouraging
crime. Although the scholarship of the twentieth century has
accustomed us to consider definitions of deviance in a sociological framework, the lengths to which these middle-class
reformers were willing to go in reproducing an image of themselves in "unfortunate" children is indeed striking. One did
not have to be clean and neat, correct and patient to stay
within the law; one did not have to protect the state in order
to stay out of its jails. The Reverend Malcolm Dana saw the
rehabilitation of wayward youth as an occasion for a probation
officer to become "practically a member of the family, and by
lessons in cleanliness, and decency, of truth and integrity
. . . he can transform the entire family into something the
State need not be ashamed to own as its citizens."[20] In such
declarations of purpose, the reformers exhibited a desire not
simply to improve upon the criminal justice system but to
retrain the child offender and his family in life patterns that
were more acceptable to the middle class.

The dual role of the juvenile court system—a humanitarian gesture toward the downtrodden and a means of con-
solidating and protecting the safety and status of the more
fortunate—is characteristic of reform as opposed to revolu-
tionary movements, and many of the reform activities that

occupied progressives exhibited the same duality. As Roy Lubove points out in his work on tenement-house reform, the miserable conditions of slum life prodded reformers into action not only because slums represented objective violations of universal standards of decency but also because they made the values of the middle class impossible to achieve.[21] The temperance movement aimed to rescue mankind from hideous dependence on alcohol as well as to ensure the reliability and productiveness of the work force. The public-health reformers exhibited solicitude for the physical condition of the poor *and* reflected the desire to protect the native population from contamination by unhealthy alien peoples.[22] The work of people interested in the process by which immigrants entered American life vacillated between the celebration of "immigrant gifts," of pluralism, and the anxious desire to remake foreigners in the safe and familiar image of Americans. The birth-control movement tried to provide individual families with the means of controlling their own destinies, but also sometimes seemed to provide the means by which the dominant middle class might preserve itself from the rampant fecundity of the lower orders, native and foreign.[23]

It is not mere conjecture to see similarly in the juvenile court movement elements of class and ethnic antagonism or of an effort to avoid them. According to the movement's own analysis, parental attitudes and home environment constituted the prime forces in molding a child's character. Also, according to that formula, "most of the children who come before the court are, naturally, the children of the poor."[24]

Responsibility for delinquency lay with the social and economic conditions of the lower class—conditions from which the reformers could easily sense their separateness. The men in the movement were usually lawyers, often judges, sometimes doctors and clergymen; the women, often well but less well educated and married to members of the same social status, were sufficiently free of domestic duties to devote much of their time to philanthropic causes. An awareness of their own good fortune was a virtual precondition of their efforts on behalf of others. Many saw that their mission involved crossing "that yawning chasm . . . dividing into hostile classes the rich and poor."[25] And they proposed to cross that chasm by offering delinquents and their families "those higher gifts that we are able to bestow."[26]

The reformers' sense of class differences between themselves and the objects of their philanthropy produced on occasion unconcealed disdain. Some court workers seemed convinced that no home deficient enough to produce a delinquent could command a child's—even a delinquent child's—affection. Henry Thurston, the chief probation officer of the Chicago juvenile court from 1906 to 1908, wrote about his reactions to the children and their families:

> Looking into their little faces, and watching them as they are taken away from their old unwholesome surroundings to be placed among environments that will lift them up and make them noble men and women instead of burdens upon society, one wonders how much these little ones really feel, and how deep their suffering really is when they are snatched away from home and parents.[27]

It did not seem at all likely that a delinquent would have parents worthy of love.

The theory that the cause of delinquency lay in lower-class environments, physical and cultural, translated into the practice of probation as uplifting contact between the delinquent and his social betters. Such contact was the very essence of probation at the beginning of the juvenile court movement, and probation lay at the heart of the ideal juvenile court.

What is novel about progressive attitudes toward child offenders is not the concern to mitigate class differences. Early nineteenth-century managers of the houses of refuge, as Stephen Schlossman points out, had seen their role in the lives of child offenders as inducing conformation to middle-class standards.[28] Rather, what is distinctive about the awareness of class differences in the progressive period is that the juvenile court movement contemplated not so much lifting the child out of his lower-class milieu as entering and transforming that milieu, not only for the child, but for his family, too.

The reformers' preference for returning the delinquent to his home did not jibe, at least superficially, with their conviction that the home had produced the delinquency in the first place. Nevertheless, for several reasons the reformers could live with this apparent contradiction. First, on the negative side, was their experience with institutional care as too rigid for individualized treatment and, more serious, as an environment more likely to teach the skills of criminality than good citizenship. Second, removing the child from his home in order to place him in another raised serious if not insurmountable legal, moral, and practical questions.

But the enthusiasm with which juvenile court reformers contemplated the probation system and its focus upon environmental as well as individual uplift cannot be accounted for by negative concerns about the alternatives alone. Schlossman believes that the juvenile court reformers' interest in a family setting for rehabilitative efforts was "one manifestation of a newly heightened sensitivity in the progressive period to the emotional bonds and educational possibilities in all families, even those in fairly dismal straits."[29] The faith in these possibilities is difficult to explain, since it seems to have emerged not from a belief in the growing strength and stability of family life but, on the contrary, from a concern that the family could not survive the effects of industrialization and the competition of other institutions—mainly educational and recreational—in socializing children.

It would appear that somehow progressive faith in the potential of family life outstripped the fear that the reality of family life was in decline. Juvenile delinquency was to provide an occasion to rejuvenate the family, and the rejuvenated family was to be an "ally"[30] in the reformation of the delinquent. Such optimism characterized to a remarkable degree the attitude of juvenile court reformers to the task of rehabilitation. The literature of the juvenile court movement contained many brief statements or summaries of the regenera-

tion process, often presenting the task as one of impressive
and even inspiring simplicity.

> There is such a thing as an instantaneous awakening of the
> soul to the realization of higher and better things by the
> magnetic influence of one soul reacting upon another.[31]

Thus, the process might have been as elementary as placing
the delinquent in touch with a law-abiding citizen, or as
simple as reasoning with him. Judge Lindsey wrote:

> We never release a boy on probation until he is impressed
> with the idea that he must obey. It is explained what the con-
> sequences will be if he does not obey and keep his word. It is
> kindly, but firmly, impressed why all this is so, and why after
> all it is for him we are working and not against him. We
> arouse his sense of responsibility.[32]

Lindsey seemed to suggest that hostility to society and its laws
was just an error of judgment, a mistake that the child would
recognize and correct if only someone took the trouble to point
it out to him. This typical statement resembles an argument
about madness made by a character in Dostoevsky's *Crime
and Punishment*:

> In Paris they have been conducting serious experiments as to
> the possibility of curing the insane, simply by logical argu-
> ment. . . . The idea is that there's really nothing wrong
> with the physical organism of the insane, and that insanity is,
> so to say, a logical mistake, an error of judgment, an incorrect
> view of things.[33]

This view of insanity implied that there existed a standard
of reason not only universal in meaning but universally
powerful in its appeal. The child-study movement took a
similar position when it suggested that an appreciation of accepted morality inhered universally in human beings. The
assumption that such standards of behavior had a natural hold
on all human beings appeared subtly in many juvenile court

articles. The superintendent of the Indiana Reform School for Boys told the National Conference of Charities and Correction in 1902:

> We must place our boy under the guidance of an affable, firm, prudent master who will help by his own example. The courteous replies and gentlemanly ways of an officer have a tendency to draw as a magnet the respect and admiration of a boy.[34]

The reformers assumed that the child offender had a "smoldering ambition" to be like the good men and women who worked for the court,[35] that he had within him all the while the potential and the desire to be an upstanding citizen, and that he needed only the example of "discreet persons of good moral character" to transform that potential into reality.

Only the assumption that accepted behavioral codes were inherent in the child could have explained the confidence with which the reformers contemplated the probation system. As originally conceived, probation treatment consisted of visits from a probation officer to the child and reports to the court by the child himself or by the probation officer. The visits and reports constituted the entire probation system, "the keystone which supports the arch of the juvenile law,"[36] the "cord upon which all the pearls of the juvenile court are strung."[37] The reformers expected the probation officer to show tact and patience and common sense, but they did not expect him to have professional skill or training. As with the judge, personal qualities mattered most. "The probation process is a process of education by constructive friendship."[38] "The friendly side of the probation officer's work is the important side."[39]

> There is no more potent influence over a boy than a good man or woman. . . . The way to make a good boy is to rub him against a good man.[40]

By expecting a casual, friendly relationship between a delinquent and a more fortunate adult to solve the child's behavioral problems, the reformers revealed a singular faith in the powers of spontaneous moral regeneration.

Thus, for all their concern about delinquency, the reformers' picture of the problem was rather rosy: whereas the child offender was clearly atypical in that he did not abide by the moral code natural to man, he was readily returned to normality; whereas for the moment he presented society with a problem, he would soon count as one of society's assets. Whatever his impulses toward crime and destruction, they were not basic, for as a normal human being his basic impulses by definition led him to preserve the social order.

The invention of the juvenile court was largely the work of the old middle class responding to one of the urban problems which troubled people in the 1890's, particularly after the panic of 1893. In a sense their response resembles what Wiebe would have considered an effort to imitate in the impersonal, urban world the informal patterns of social control which belonged to disappearing village life. The reformers' hope that disinterested observers in the community would petition the juvenile court on behalf of children is one point of resemblance. The importance of a fatherly judge in face-to-face contact with the children and their families is another. The initial commitment to volunteer probation service by people whose main qualification for the work was their social status is a third. As Geoffrey C. Hazard, Jr., has recently written, "It often seems that juvenile law is operating on an unarticulated wish that young people would behave as though they were members of an integrated and static society living in untroubled times."[41]

On the other hand, the institution that this old middle class invented embodied much of what is characteristic of progressivism. It invited the kind of administration by the kind of people—the new middle class—which Wiebe associates with progressivism and Brown associates with modernization. While the emphasis on a judge with personal involvement in his work seems to have been genuine and to have endured, it also demanded specialization in juvenile court work. The emphasis on a personal approach in probation was clearly less enduring and probably made a virtue of necessity—the political necessity to avoid burdening juvenile court proposals with expensive probation systems, and the more mundane necessity to get along with amateurs, since social work itself had not yet become a profession and the social sciences were only just emerging. When social work did become professional and the social sciences became better developed, there was already a place for them in the juvenile court system.

The emphasis of the earliest reformers on the importance of "social" testimony in juvenile cases made that place. The vagueness of definitions of delinquency had moved the decision as to what a delinquent was out of the legislature, which made the criminal law, and into the court. The lack of a time limit, except the achievement of majority, on dispositions in juvenile court gave full scope to the discretion of specialists who from the moment of petition (and even without one) had flexible, continuous control. This scope was augmented by the disinclination to institutionalize children: children who went to reform schools passed out of the control of the juvenile court: children who went home on probation did not. Juvenile courts, unfettered by the rules of criminal procedure, took delinquency out of the adversary process much as other progressive reforms took issues out of the contentious, unpredictable world of electoral politics.

Although the founders of the juvenile court did not fit comfortably into the new middle class to which Wiebe attributes progressivism, and although in its first manifestation the juvenile court idea had aspects which also make the fit not quite perfect, Wiebe himself counts the juvenile court among progressive institutions. He associates it with developments in law generally which tended to replace fixed rules with processes that adapted better to shifting contingencies. He associates it, correctly, with the emergence of sociological jurisprudence "which would adjust legal decisions to inductive, social evidence."[42]

That some aspects of the movement appear "conservative" because they emphasized social control and drew upon experiments already made, and that other aspects appear "reformist" because they emphasized the rehabilitative ideal and found new ways to pursue it, ought not to mystify us. As F. A. Allen has said, "No institution as complex as the juvenile court emerges suddenly and fully formed."[43] And the juvenile court reformers like most reformers were anxious to prove both that they had discovered something new which should be tried and that the trial would not be overly risky because it was related in spirit or form to tradition. It is also characteristic of the reformer, almost by definition, that he seeks to eliminate abuses in the system while preserving the system in its fundamentals. No one should be surprised to find in a reform program, particularly in the realm of penology, signs of such conservatism. Given the inherently double nature of reform movements, it makes little sense to seize excitedly upon one aspect or the other as its essence. This is as true of progressivism in general as it is of the juvenile court movement in particular.

That the juvenile court movement made an easy fit with progressivism is clear from its reception. The juvenile court idea was received as the height of social justice and "was one of the most popular innovations in an era renowned for its solicitous attention to children."[44] Optimism for the fulfillment of its promise pervaded the movement as it pervaded all of the progressive era.

3

THE LEGAL SETTING

However intent reformers were upon the social or therapeutic nature of the juvenile court, and however successful in expunging from its language the vocabulary of criminal law, the juvenile court was and is a legal institution. As the therapeutic ambitions of the court have come into question, its legal nature has appeared in starker relief: developments in the definition of due process both in criminal and in civil commitment proceedings have made the novel combination of criminal and civil concepts in the juvenile court seem both isolated and peculiar. But even to understand what the juvenile court reformers were about in their own time and to understand the contemporary acceptance of their program, it is helpful to locate the juvenile court in its legal and jurisprudential setting.

From the vantage point of the late twentieth century, the temptation is to contrast the juvenile court with criminal courts and to be somewhat shocked by the deprivation of defendants' rights in juvenile court. What seems most peculiar about the juvenile court to the late-twentieth-century mind is its fusion of a definition of delinquency which depends heavily on the criminal code with a procedure that depends heavily on the civil tradition.

It is, however, something of an anachronism to hold the juvenile court reformers up to the light of due process values as they have come to be associated with the Constitution over the course of the twentieth century. For in their pursuit of the dual ends of greater protection for society and greater solicitude for the child offender, the reformers were relatively unimpeded by contemporary commitment to due process of law as we now understand it. The phase "due process of law" existed, of course, in the Constitution then as now, but the meaning of that phrase and the relative importance attached to it—as opposed to other values involved in the criminal process—have changed. The Warren Court would not have evoked such intense controversy were this not so.

Herbert Packer has created, for the sake of analysis, two models of the criminal process, both of which are ideal types and neither of which exists in reality in pure form.[1] The "due process" model tries to keep the criminal justice system as open-ended as possible and to give the accused every opportunity to acquit himself. It allows for the likelihood that errors will be committed in the administration of justice and requires the correction of such errors before there can be a conviction, even if the facts point to a guilty verdict. Although it is certainly concerned with the repression of crime, the due process model would prefer to see the machinery of the state stall than to allow it to churn out convictions by procedures which violate the rights of defendants. Given the inequality between the resources of the prosecution and of the defense, and given the consequences of conviction, the due process model enshrines procedural safeguards as essential to general liberty.

By the middle of the twentieth century, these values were quite closely associated with the federal Constitution. But many of the rules that came to constitute requisite parts of the meaning of due process were formulated and applied to the states by the Supreme Court only after the Second World War, and some of them only in the 1960's. The rules of evidence, the right to counsel, the Eighth Amendment provision for bail, the protection against self-incrimination, the right to appeal, all underwent major redefinitions and had to be "found" in the due process clause of the Fourteenth

Amendment before they could be required in their redefinitions to apply to state courts, where most criminal cases are heard. Indeed, one of the most difficult issues of constitutional litigation in the twentieth century has been whether and to what degree the Fourteenth Amendment incorporates the Bill of Rights and constrains the states to treat criminal defendants in particular ways.

To take but one example, the right to counsel has undergone several metamorphoses in its constitutional meaning during the twentieth century, not all of them expansive. When the Scottsboro boys were convicted of raping two girls on a train, the appeal, which came to the Supreme Court as *Powell v. Alabama*[2] in 1932, raised a novel question. Was it a violation of the due process clause of the Fourteenth Amendment for the trial court to have failed to afford the defendants "a fair opportunity to secure counsel of their own choice," and to have made a designation of counsel "either so indefinite or so close upon the trial as to amount to a denial of effective and substantial aid . . ."?[3] The Court held that both were deprivations of due process, given the facts of the case. The defendants were young and ignorant, isolated from friends and family, exposed to intense local hostility and, significantly, to a death penalty. In holding that the trial court's belated provision of ineffective counsel constituted a denial of due process, the Court changed the meanings of due process and the right to counsel in at least a limited number of capital cases. The dissent of Mr. Justice Butler criticized the majority for finding any deprivation of federal rights in the case and particularly for finding in the federal Constitution not only a right to secure counsel oneself but also a right to effective appointment of counsel in state courts. This he said was "an extension of federal authority into a field hitherto occupied exclusively by the several States."[4]

It is remarkable that in *Powell* the Supreme Court for the first time reversed a state criminal conviction for procedural unfairness.[5] As late as 1932, a landmark decision was required to settle the question whether the right to counsel was sufficiently fundamental to fairness in the adversary process to extend to state proceedings through the Fourteenth Amendment. And then, in 1942, *Powell* was followed by *Betts v. Brady,* and it became clear that the question had not been settled at all. Betts had been charged with robbery in a county of Maryland where, though he was indigent, he was denied appointed counsel because the practice there was to provide counsel only in murder and rape cases. He was convicted and imprisoned. His petition for a writ of *habeas corpus,* seeking release on the ground that he had been denied his right to counsel in violation of the Fourteenth Amendment, was turned down. The Supreme Court, leaning heavily on the aspect of *Powell* that emphasized the facts and circumstances of a particular case, decided in review that the "appointment of counsel is not a fundamental right, essential to a fair trial" in every circumstance, and affirmed the denial of the writ.[6] Although the Sixth Amendment came to require counsel in all *federal* criminal proceedings, it was not until 1963, in *Gideon v. Wainwright,*[7] that the Court held squarely that the right to counsel—appointed if necessary—was a fundamental right and essential to a fair trial, not just in special circumstances, but in all criminal trials. Even then, major questions concerning the scope of this right remained. Realizing that *Gideon* was decided in 1963 makes us somewhat less shocked that, in 1967 for the first time, the Supreme Court held that juveniles and their parents had a right to counsel in delinquency proceedings which might lead to commitment; that they must be notified of their right to retain counsel and, if unable to retain counsel themselves, have the assistance of appointed counsel.[8]

This is not to say that defendants in state criminal proceedings had no protections before the landmark decisions of the Warren Court. It is to say only that the refined meanings of those protections and the preoccupation with them that characterized the Supreme Court in the 1960's did not characterize the legal mind as it applied itself to criminal proceedings in the late nineteenth or early twentieth century. On the contrary, Packer suggests that another model of law-enforcement values, which he calls the crime control model, has dominated the actual operations of police and prosecutors, and has also, at various times in our history, dominated the thinking of our most highly respected jurists.

This set of values holds that the sole aim of the law-enforcement apparatus is the apprehension and punishment of criminals. Its purpose is to punish offenders so that they will not repeat the offense and so that others will be deterred from committing it. In this view, law enforcement is the only guarantee of social freedom, and the key to the system is its certainty. Unlike the due process model which would, in the familiar phrase, prefer that a hundred guilty men go free rather than one innocent man be convicted, the crime control model holds that, in order for society to be protected, the law must be enforced with absolute certainty, and none must escape without punishment. Placing its faith in the accuracy of the law-enforcement apparatus, it presumes that the accused is guilty, not innocent.

For this reason, the crime control model distrusts the adversary procedure which dominates American criminal prosecutions. In such procedure it is possible for a clever lawyer to save a guilty client either by swaying the jury and the judge or by appealing on some procedural technicality. The more rules that surround the criminal process, the more likely, of course, that a procedural violation will occur, a conviction will be reversed, and a guilty person will go free.

The best possible outcome of the pre-trial sequence for the crime control model is for the defendant to enter a plea of guilty, so that the machinery of the adversary system need never start turning at all. In mid-twentieth century, as jurists moved closer to the due process model, law-enforcement officials who shared crime control values continued to strive to remove the obstacles which due process put in the way of convictions. At the time of the creation of juvenile courts not only law-enforcement officials but legal thinkers as well were more sensitive to the demands of crime control than to the dangers of violating due process.

Richard M. Brown, in discussing the genesis of American vigilante movements, has pointed out the affinity between

Packer's crime control model of law-enforcement values and the attitudes of leading legal minds of the late nineteenth century.[9] The response of these minds to the resurgence of vigilantism in that period illustrates this affinity. Sometimes reluctantly and despairingly, sometimes enthusiastically, many legal figures recommended solutions to the threat of vigilantism which implicitly adopted some of the values of short-cut vigilante justice. Instead of insisting on the punishment of people who took the law into their own hands, they suggested ways to make formal justice more swift, final, and satisfying to the public desire for retribution.

Roscoe Pound, one of America's greatest writers on the law, concluded that adversary procedure, with its delays and opportunities for evasion, discredited the law by inviting defendants to beat it, and also discredited it by frustrating the public's legitimate desire for safety.[10] Others suggested an end to the executive's power of pardon, restriction of the right to appeal, and the elimination of the jury system with its opportunities for corruption. Among the advocates of such anti-due-process notions were Supreme Court Justices David Brewer and Stephen Field, justices of state supreme courts, and other legal illuminati.

In 1890, Charles Bonaparte, who would become Theodore Roosevelt's Secretary of the Navy and U.S. Attorney General (and president of the Union for Doing Good), made the following remarks at the Yale Law School: "It is of course an evil that the law should occasionally be enforced by lawless means, but it is in my opinion a GREATER EVIL that it should be habitually duped and evaded by means formally lawful."[11] Oliver Wendell Holmes, Jr., wrote in 1881:

> The first requirement of a sound body of law is that it should correspond with the actual feelings and demands of the community, whether right or wrong. If people would gratify the passion of revenge outside the law, the law has no choice but to satisfy the craving itself, and thus avoid the greater evil of private retribution.[12]

In the late nineteenth century, when the meaning of due process and its application to state proceedings were less fully delineated, and when the adversary system was under attack from legal scholars as sometimes unworkable and itself an obstruction of justice, it was much easier than it would have been sixty years later to suggest for the first time the creation of a court for children which eliminated procedural safeguards awarded to defendants by the Bill of Rights. But if there was less to lose by the elimination of criminal safeguards in 1899 than there is now, there was still something to lose. While children remained largely subject to the same legal sanctions for the same offenses as adults, they also enjoyed the same procedural rights, however underdeveloped. And it was to be expected that children would bring constitutional challenges to the juvenile court laws that divested them of those rights.

The most common defense against such challenges, and the dominant theory of the juvenile court, was that the new institution derived not from the criminal law tradition but from the common law doctrine of *parens patriae*. According to that doctrine, the King of England was the ultimate parent and guardian of all the children within his realm and was therefore responsible, acting through the chancellor's court, for the care of all children who needed his protection. Juvenile court reformers explained that the function of *parens patriae* had passed from the King of England to the governments of the several states after the American Revolution, and that juvenile court statutes simply placed the function in a new court. In 1910, Bernard Flexner, a lawyer who wrote a good deal about the legal aspect of the juvenile court, explained the principle of the juvenile court and its relationship to British precedent:

> The child . . . henceforth shall be viewed as the ward of the state, to be cared for by it, and not as any enemy of the state, to be punished by it. . . . This principle is not new; on the contrary it is old, and it is found in many of the early English Chancery cases.[13]

Charles Henderson, a past president of the National Conference of Charities and Correction, wrote in 1904:

> Our country has inherited the English law and our courts of various name have inherited the powers of the ancient Court of Chancery which enable them to enforce the duties of parents and to protect the rights of infants. Our judges have recently discovered in these principles very large and unsuspected powers and have used them.[14]

The *parens patriae* theory was thought to place the juvenile court and its treatment of child offenders securely in a long chain of legal precedent.

The doctrine of *parens patriae* had served American juvenile justice reformers before. The doctrine was crucial to the operation of juvenile reformatories during the nineteenth century, for it legitimized the incarceration there of noncriminal youth.[15] In 1838, the doctrine served to deny the *habeas corpus* petition of Mary Ann Crouse for release from the Philadelphia House of Refuge, where she had been sent on the complaint of her mother by a justice of the peace. Without being charged with any crime and without a jury trial, a child could be incarcerated until she reached majority as an appropriate exercise of the state's function as *parens patriae*.[16]

There were, however, several problems involved in the theory that the doctrine explained and served as precedent for the juvenile court. While it was true that the court of chancery had carried out the King's function of ultimate parent, it had usually done so only if the child in question had property. Critics frequently pointed to this fact as an obstacle to the legitimate creation of juvenile courts based on the chancery model. Defenders of the chancery model had a ready answer in the decision of Lord Eldon in the Wellesley case of 1827, which asserted that it was for want of the means of exercising its jurisdiction over unpropertied children, not for want of jurisdiction itself that the court of chancery had confined its exercise of the role of *parens patriae* to children with property. Juvenile court reformers argued that in both English and American law, once the means were available either through public funds or through legal enforcement of parental duties, the courts could exercise fully the powers of the chancery courts over all children.

A more serious—indeed ostensibly crucial—problem for the advocates of the chancery theory of juvenile court origins lay in the ancient distinction between dependent or neglected children and children who had offended against the law. The court of chancery had assumed jurisdiction over children who needed protection. This category included children who had been abandoned or abused or whose rights had been violated; it did not include children who had committed crimes. In fact, children above the age of criminal responsibility (fixed traditionally at age seven) might be punished in the criminal courts exactly as adults were punished for the same offenses. The perceived inappropriateness of this situation had contributed to interest in the reform of juvenile justice: the law grouped child offenders with adult criminals when it should have grouped them with other unfortunate children. The doctrine of *parens patriae* had served in cases like Mary Ann Crouse's to group noncriminal children with criminal children in reformatories and thus to blur the distinctions in treatment between them. But for children convicted of crime, the state had functioned as ultimate parent through institutional treatment *after* commitment by the criminal courts. The proposal of chancery procedure in the courtroom to deal with delinquents accused of criminal acts significantly advanced the principle that the state had to take a "protective" role with a class of people from which society had traditionally received protection.

The proponents of the juvenile court ideal realized that they were applying chancery approaches to a class of children to which they had not been applied before. Indeed, the obliteration of distinctions between delinquent children and dependent or neglected children was the explicit aim of the juvenile court movement. It was admitted that juvenile court legislation "undertakes to apply to the delinquent child the same procedure it would apply to the neglected child."[17] Julian Mack, juvenile court judge in Chicago from 1904 to

1907, put this change at the center of the new institution's definition:

> What we did not have [before the juvenile court laws] was the concept that a child that broke the law was to be dealt with by the State as a wise parent would deal with a wayward child.[18]

The belief that the delinquent resembled the dependent in that each had suffered at the hand of society, and that both therefore needed the protection of the state, motivated efforts to withdraw the child offender from the arena of the criminal courts and submit him to the more flexible inquiry of courts constituted on the chancery model.

In discussing the origins of the juvenile court, many who proposed that delinquents be equated with dependents attempted to minimize the novelty of this change. One of the early histories of the juvenile court movement concluded that the extension of the doctrine of *parens patriae* to proceedings for children who broke the criminal code "has been generally accepted merely as a logical extension of the principle of chancery and of guardianship which was applied in the court of chancery."[19]

In fact, this "logical" extension viewed legally, rather than as a variation on a theme of juvenile justice reform, was a distinct novelty. From the perspective of defendants' rights, it could not be regarded as "merely" change in degree.

In all those cases which challenged the juvenile court on due process grounds, there was one key issue: would the courts of appeal accept what the legislation and its proponents contended: that the proceedings in juvenile court derived from chancery rather than criminal law origins; that they aimed at the protection and best interests rather than the punishment of the child; that they constituted therefore a special class of civil cases to which right to jury trial, counsel, and appeal, and perhaps even the rules of evidence and standards of proof did not apply? If so, the juvenile courts could justifiably replace traditional procedural safeguards against the power of the state with a new set of protections against inadequate family and community surroundings.

Few courts of review had difficulty accepting the proposition that juvenile court proceedings were civil simply when the legislation said they were. In 1908, the Michigan Supreme Court in *Robison v. Wayne Circuit Judges*[20] regretfully declared the juvenile court act of Detroit invalid on the ground that it had all the elements of a criminal trial, including the imposition of fines, but did not honor the right to trial by a jury of twelve. The decision was, however, an exception to the general rule of rapid and total acceptance of the reasoning and rhetoric of the juvenile court movement. The courts of appeals held that the juvenile court statutes did not violate children's rights by eliminating safeguards included in criminal procedure because juvenile court proceedings were not trials to determine criminal guilt and did not dispense punishment. In 1905, the decision in *Commonwealth v. Fisher*[21] expressed the classic rationale of juvenile court procedure: "The court passes upon nothing but the propriety of an effort to save [the child]. . . . The very purpose of the act is to prevent a trial." The Pennsylvania juvenile court act, the opinion maintained, did not violate defendants' rights because: "The design is not punishment nor the restraint imprisonment, any more than is the wholesome restraint which a parent exercises over his child."[22] The Idaho decision in *In Re Sharp* concluded that juvenile court dispositions were not deprivations of liberty without due process because the child's right to liberty was attenuated at best:

> It would be carrying the protection of "inalienable rights," guaranteed by the Constitution, a long way to say that that guarantee extends to a free and unlimited exercise of the whims, caprices or proclivities of a child . . . for idleness, ignorance, crime, indigence, or any kindred disposition.[23]

Whereas adults might have a right to liberty, children had only a right to custody which the juvenile court vindicated rather than deprived in taking over the parental function.

Distinctions between criminal and noncriminal behavior, between parental and state discipline, disappeared in the cloud
of *parens patriae* doctrine:

> To save a child from becoming a criminal, or from continuing
> a career of crime, . . . the legislature may surely provide for
> the salvation of such a child, if its parents or guardian be un-
> able or unwilling to do so, by bringing it into one of the
> courts of the state *without any process at all* for the purpose of
> subjecting it to the state's guardianship and protection. . . .
> The act simply provides how children who ought to be saved
> may reach the court to be saved. If experience should show
> that there ought to be other ways for it to get there, the legis-
> lature can, and undoubtedly will, adopt them, and *they will
> never be regarded as undue processes for depriving a child of
> its liberty* or property as a penalty for a crime committed.[24]
> [Emphasis mine]

American judges put their faith in the good intentions of
the juvenile court movement and in the capacity of the court
to carry out the role of ultimate parent. Against this faith, the
complaints on behalf of children that their constitutional
rights were in jeopardy made no headway. And the challenges
to juvenile court laws brought by parents who asserted their
custodial rights in their children were no more successful.
The intervention of the juvenile court in the lives of delinquent children was justified by the twin observations of the
misbehavior of the children and the unfitness of their parents
to correct it. We have already seen that the courts of review
accepted without difficulty the reformers' indifference to procedures designed to prove the misbehavior of the children
beyond a reasonable doubt; they were similarly accepting of
laxness in demonstrating factually the unfitness of the
parents.

Roman and common law had long protected the rights and
authority of parents over their children. While the more extreme parental prerogatives disappeared from the Anglo-
American legal tradition, the parents' right to custody and to
the value of a child's labor endured. Parents continued to

control the education and religious affiliations of their children, to arrange and veto marriages of children below a certain age, and to transfer custody of their children to other adults and institutions without the intervention of the state. There remained much in American law which served to bolster rather than interfere with the authority of parents. The Connecticut legal code of 1672 provided that children over sixteen who cursed or struck their parents could be put to death unless the behavior was justified by "very unchristianly neglect in the education of such children" or by the child's need to defend himself against death or maiming through extremely cruel parental correction. In 1819, Illinois put itself behind parental authority by passing a law which provided that children who disobeyed their parents might be sent to jail or to a house of correction. Other nineteenth-century reformatories were available to receive children whose parents found them difficult to control.

The privileges of parental status of course brought concomitant responsibilities. Parents had to provide the necessities of life for their children, and to allow for their education. It has long been illegal for a parent to abandon a child who cannot maintain himself. But the sanctions attached to a failure to perform these duties have never constituted a significant threat: neighbors are loath to invite authorities to invade the privacy of neighbors, and children are ill equipped intellectually, emotionally, and financially to challenge parents in courts of law. Even in those cases where inadequacy shaded into overt abuse, it was unlikely that a parent's failure would come to the attention of the authorities, and even when it did, a child could not recover damages. The right to custody was enforced far more often than the corresponding obligations.

Nevertheless, growing concern for children and childhood in the early nineteenth century began to moderate the power of parents. In the United States the courts stated explicitly that the right of a parent to custody of his child was not inalienable, and could be forfeited by failure to perform the duties which correspond to his rights.[25] Those who wanted to protect children from their parents sometimes used arguments which suggested a contract theory of parenthood. Far from being a primary and immutable relationship, the argument went, the arrangement between parent and child was the creation of the state, which granted custody to natural parents only because this was the most efficient and convenient arrangement. If a parent's treatment of his child violated legal standards, the relationship ceased to satisfy the state's conditions and custody *reverted* to the state as ultimate parent.

Whatever the historical validity of such propositions, when translated into legal procedure, they would seem to call for some demonstration that the parent had indeed failed to live up to the hypothetical contract and had thereby forfeited his rights in his child. In 1897, before the passage of California's juvenile court act, the supreme court of that state ruled in *Ex Parte Becknell*[26] that "parents cannot be deprived of their right to their child's care, custody, society, and service except by a proceeding to which they are made parties and in which it is shown that they are unfit or unwilling or unable to perform their parental duties."

The apparent fairness of this ruling notwithstanding, it did not govern the conduct of cases in juvenile courts either in California or elsewhere. Few juvenile court laws required an investigation into the fitness of the parents as a condition of the removal of the child either to an institution or to another home. In most states the juvenile court judge could transfer a delinquent to the custody of a state officer in any case he deemed appropriate. Under most laws "it [was] sufficient to show a condition of delinquency on the part of the child and it [was] not necessary to prove the failure on the part of the parents. . . ."[27] In such a system the delinquency of the child constituted a *prima facie* case against the parent which the parent had little opportunity to contest formally. Or, as a recent decision has stated, "The best interest of the child and the fitness of his parents are not necessarily inter-dependent.[28] The earliest juvenile court laws did not even afford parents the simpler aspect of the safeguard intended by the *Becknell* decision—notification of parents by the court of proceedings involving their children.

Occasionally a court of review balked at the treatment of custodial rights by juvenile courts. In *Mill v. Brown*,[29] the Utah Supreme Court in 1907 released a child from a reformatory because there had been no independent judgment that his parents were so derelict in their duties as to forfeit their custodial rights. The court stated that "unless . . . both the delinquency of the child and the incompetency . . . of the parent concur, and are so found, the court exceeds its power" when transferring custody out of the home. Nevertheless, most of the decisions regarding parents' rights required only that parents be notified of the proceedings against their children and did not question transfers of custody which took place without demonstration of parental inadequacy and without parental consent. Thus, the doctrine of *parens patriae* furthered the attenuation of parental rights as it swept into the procedurally lax domain of the juvenile courts those children who would have otherwise been been tried at criminal law.

Even at the time of greatest activity in the creation of juvenile courts, there were those who doubted that *parens patriae* theory accounted for the jurisdiction and proceedings of the new institution with respect to those delinquent children who had committed acts which would be criminal if committed by adults. Those who remained dissatisfied with this legal justification were more likely to be judges and lawyers than lay supporters of the movement. They believed that to treat such children to the solicitude rather than the wrath of the community represented the consolidation of a revolution in attitudes toward children and crime, and that chancery theory did more to describe than to analyze or justify it. Those who were sympathetic to the result but dissatisfied with the explanation offered another theory of the legal origins of the juvenile court.

They sought instead to find the roots of the juvenile court's approach to child offenders in the traditions of the criminal law itself. They turned to the ancient distinction made in criminal law between those who could be held legally responsible for their acts, because they were capable of criminal intent, and those who could not be held responsible, because they were incapable of criminal intent. One of the criteria for making this distinction was insanity; another was age. Roman, French, and English law had long assumed that children under the age of seven were incapable of criminal intent; American criminal law assumed that a child between the ages of seven and fourteen was also incapable of criminal intent unless the prosecution established that a particular child had sufficient intelligence and maturity to have understood his own behavior. Those who considered the juvenile court an application of this time-honored distinction argued that juvenile court laws had merely extended the age through which a child was automatically considered incapable of criminal intent, usually until the age of sixteen. Where the *parens patriae* theory seemed to beg the question of why children who broke the criminal code should not answer for their acts before a criminal court, this explanation seemed to answer the question from the criminal law itself. The juvenile court, it suggested, was an expansion of the defense of infancy.

But was this an accurate representation of the changes wrought by the juvenile court? If so, if the juvenile court had merely advanced the age through which a child was presumed incapable of criminal intent, the new court should have been treating fifteen-year-old offenders as the criminal law treated six-year-olds—that is, by acquitting for reasons of infancy. The explanation from the analogy with the defense of infancy explained why children were not to be punished in criminal court for criminal code violations; it did not explain why such children should have to answer for their behavior in some other court. Juvenile court reformers did seem to be arguing that children were incapable of criminal intent in the manner of true infants, but in fact they were proposing to treat child offenders as if they had resorted to the defense of insanity.

In criminal law, the state must prove beyond a reasonable doubt a number of independent "elements" of a crime. For example, in the case of a murder by shooting, the state must prove not only that the victim was shot and died from the wound, and that the accused fired the gun that discharged the bullet that killed him, but that the accused intended to kill. This last material element of guilty mind, or *mens rea,* is the element which was intended to sort out of the criminal process people whom it seemed unfair or unwise to subject to criminal sanctions because they did not or could not freely choose to do the evil they did. If there was no guilty mind, there was no crime. Even if the state could prove all these elements, including *mens rea,* beyond a reasonable doubt, the defendant might still be acquitted if he could set up a defense such as self-protection or police entrapment.

Jay Katz and Joseph Goldstein have pointed out that before the M'Naghten case in 1843, evidence concerning mental state, of capacity to judge right from wrong, went to the question of the presence of *mens rea.*[30] This evidence, by suggesting that one of the material elements was missing, raised the question whether a crime had been committed at all, rather than raising a defense to a crime all the material elements of which were present. Because the accused could secure acquittal by bringing evidence of insanity to bear on the issue of guilty mind, Katz and Goldstein suggest that from the point of view of the defendant there was no need for the insanity "defense" which got its start in the M'Naghten case.

In fact, the M'Naghten insanity defense and the variations which have been played on its theme have a very different effect from testimony that throws *mens rea* into question and from all other "defenses." If one disproves the presence of criminal intent, one goes free. If one concedes the presence of all the material elements of a crime, but successfully establishes the defense of self-preservation, one goes free. In neither case does the state continue to interfere in one's life. But if one raises the "defense" of insanity one doesn't go to jail, but one does go to a mental institution for an indefinite period of time.

Katz and Goldstein conclude that the effect—indeed the purpose—of the insanity defense is not to absolve from criminal liability those who were beyond rational self-control, since the concept of *mens rea* was already available as a vehicle for exempting the insane from criminal sanctions. On the contrary, the effect and purpose of the insanity defense, they say, are to subject to indeterminate restraint those who would otherwise have been altogether free of it. It is designed, they conclude, to authorize the holding of persons who have, according to traditional concepts of criminal law, committed no crime.[31] The restraint to which they would be subject was not, to be sure, the restraint which criminal sanctions would provide. Their restraint was to be treatment in a mental hospital, but they were not to have their freedom.

Juvenile court legislation had a similar, if less direct effect on juveniles accused of having committed an act which in an adult would be criminal. Before the passage of juvenile court legislation, a child under seven was conclusively presumed to be incapable of criminal intent. A child between seven and fourteen was also presumed to be free of a guilty mind unless the prosecution could prove unusual maturity. Had the purpose of the juvenile court laws simply been to exculpate all children and shield them from criminal sanctions, the appropriate vehicle would have been to extend the age below which a child was conclusively presumed to be without *mens rea* or, more moderately, at least to extend the age below which the state had to overcome such presumption by proving sufficient maturity beyond a reasonable doubt. Or, another legal route to the same end would have been to establish the defense of "youth" or "immaturity" which might have been raised after the concession of *mens rea* to achieve acquittal if the intent were simply to protect children from criminal sanctions. But such was not the intent of the juvenile court laws: while the reformers did indeed wish to remove children from the ambit of the criminal law, they did not wânt to let them go. While they *said* that children were incapable of criminal intent and that that was the reason for civil jurisdiction, the effect of that civil jurisdiction (of that metaphorical "defense" of immaturity) was, like the insanity defense, to authorize the restraint and control of people who, according to the concepts of criminal law, were not guilty of a crime.

On very rare occasions, the similarity between the criminal law's treatment of the insane and the juvenile court's treatment of child offenders came through explicitly. A participant at the National Conference of Charities and Correction said in 1902: "It is hard that children should be brought into court for 'committing a crime.' A child cannot commit a crime: they are in the same class as the insane in this respect."[32] The similarity may be more apparent from our vantage point than from theirs. Nevertheless, the attitude of juvenile court reformers to child offenders exhibits more than a little resemblance to attitudes toward the insane, including the ambivalence which Katz and Goldstein notice behind the insanity defense:

> What must be recognized is the enormous ambivalence toward the "sick" reflected in conflicting wishes to exculpate and to blame; to sanction and not to sanction; to degrade and to elevate; to stigmatize and not stigmatize; to care and to reject; to treat and to mistreat; to protect and to destroy.[33]

The partial resemblance of the juvenile court process to the criminal law's treatment of the insane, to chancery jurisdiction over dependent and neglected children, and to the concepts of the relevance of age to criminal proceedings illustrates that there were a number of legal sources from which to draw in creating a new court for children in the late nineteenth century. These resemblances and the ready acceptance of the juvenile court indicate its continuity with traditions either of law or of juvenile justice reform. But while there were precedents for blurring the distinctions between dependent and delinquent children, and while there was precedent for treating offenders differently on the basis of age or mental capacity, none of these precedents accounts for the peculiar combination of them which the juvenile court represents. The combination of them and the extension of each were novel contributions. The extensions and the combination are notable primarily for the interventionism which they authorized. To be sure, the nature of the intervention was to be "treatment" rather than punishment, and the means of intervention probation rather than the separation of children from their families, but what is striking is the ease with which juvenile court reformers secured acceptance for an institution with extraordinary legal power, and extraordinary judicial and administrative discretion on the basis of tenuous arguments from precedent.

J. Lawrence Schultz has written in an article called "The Cycle of Juvenile Court History" that procedural informality in juvenile court hearings was not a crucial part of the program of the juvenile court movement and that its acceptance was not secured by a promise of therapeutic treatment either during or after those hearings.[34] I think he is incorrect on both counts. On the first count—the question of the role procedural informality played in the treatment scheme of the juvenile court—he is misled in part by too heavy a reliance upon the testimony of judges, who would, more than any other segment of the juvenile court movement, have had respect for formal courtroom procedures. He concedes that Judge Lindsey was an exception, but he does not attend sufficiently to the reformers' repeated pleas that the juvenile court judge be freed from his elevated and formal role to come into personal contact with the children for therapeutic purposes. On the second count—the question of whether the reformers intended a *quid pro quo* which exchanged procedural safeguards for a promise of therapeutic treatment—the error is somewhat less clear. Perhaps because due process rights were less well developed and respected than they are now, and perhaps for other reasons, defenders of procedural informality in juvenile court were not called upon to make elaborate promises concerning the nature of a right to treatment in exchange for due process rights. But whereas no one may have demanded a detailed *quid pro quo* from them, and whereas they may not have intended to focus on what the juvenile court owed in exchange for the rights of defendants, the dominant chancery-origins defense of juvenile court procedure repeatedly justified the juvenile court on the basis of its nonpunitive intentions and effects. To say, as the reformers and appellate decisions did, that procedural informality was not a threat to children because the goal of juvenile court hearings was to help and protect rather than punish is to come very close indeed to making such a *quid pro quo,* even if the promise was vague about what it meant to help and protect rather than punish.

Furthermore, whether the reformers intended to bind themselves or not, it became apparent almost immediately that they had done so. Almost as soon as the ideal of the juvenile court had been embodied in real, functioning institutions, the question arose whether they were meeting the therapeutic task.

4

THE IDEAL
IN PRACTICE

By their favorable appellate review of the reform legislation, American jurists accepted the promise of the juvenile court to rehabilitate the young offender. But the ease with which the reformers secured acceptance of their promise gave no hint of the difficulty they would encounter in keeping it. The legal sensibility of the country proved far more tractable than reality.

The honeymoon of the juvenile court with the public was remarkably brief. With no more than a decade's experience behind it, the juvenile court became the subject of public investigations and newspaper campaigns.

In the years 1911 and 1912, several major cities witnessed exposés and investigations of their courts. In 1911 in Louisville, Kentucky, a group of probation officers resigned under fire. In Illinois, the birthplace of reform, the legislature passed a bill which would have done away entirely with the juvenile court system had the governor not vetoed it. Undaunted, critics of the court launched a civil-service investigation and a citizens' committee mounted another simultaneously. Newspaper stories carried charges of carelessness and neglect against probation officers. A suit was filed in Illinois superior court to secure an injunction against the children's court on the ground that it was an unconstitutional violation of the rights of parents which had been tolerated only because the clientele of the court were typically poor and helpless. Although these attacks subsided without mortal effect on the courts, they pricked the mood of self-satisfaction which had surrounded the movement and called into question the court's claim to public support.

After the first decade, the public enthusiasm which had greeted reform faded into apathy. Perhaps the initial enthusiasm itself had ensured eventual disappointment; perhaps the public had, as many observers later said, seized upon the court—as an earlier generation had seized upon reformatories —as a cure-all and had expected too much of it. Perhaps public opinion had been destined all along to swing from the purposeful generosity which had celebrated the court's ideals to a renewed fear of coddling the criminal. After World War I, which had seen another apparent increase in the adult crime rate, sentiment seemed to grow for the intensification of punishment. Some newspapers urged not only greater severity in dealing with criminals but the abolition of the parole system for adults. The combination of fear of adult criminals with revelations of practical failings in the treatment of juveniles which was supposed to prevent them from becoming adult criminals put the juvenile court on the defensive.

But just at the moment when the juvenile court needed defending, its most likely champions were also experiencing a loss of confidence. Toward the end of World War I, people professionally involved with juvenile corrections—judges, probation officers, and social scientists—began to evaluate the juvenile court experience for themselves and to come to some discouraging conclusions.

An accurate measurement of success in rehabilitative procedures has long eluded criminologists. Even measurement of the incidence of crime presents difficulties, for variation of such factors as the inclination of the police to arrest, of the judge or jury to convict, the success of criminals in evading capture—all affect the figures in constantly shifting and essentially unknowable ways. Since it is hard to know what the crime rate was at any given moment in the past, it is at least as difficult to know whether the introduction of new modes of treatment, or some other sociological factor, created a change in that rate. Even decisions as to the success or failure of work with a particular offender raise complicated questions: on what basis can it be said that he has been successfully treated; after how many years of what kind of behavior under what conditions?

Determining the results of rehabilitative efforts with juveniles presents an even greater challenge. The officers of the juvenile court in each jurisdiction have great (though varying) latitude to detain a child though his "offense" be an act of mischief, and to release another though his act be a crime. The effort to save the child's reputation often produces a fuzziness in the record which defies future analysis. Further, large but differing proportions of the court's cases are handled without benefit of judge or formal hearing, and the actual effects of the course of treatment are always confused by the powerful but untestable influence of growth, of the natural process of development which might, unassisted, have carried the child beyond the pattern of delinquency.

In spite of these difficulties, or perhaps because they had not yet come to light, the juvenile court enthusiasts of the early years made impressive claims for the success of the court's rehabilitative efforts. In 1902, the president of the New Jersey State Conference of Charities and Correction reported a large diminution in crime as a result of the use of probation with children in the juvenile courts.[1] In 1904, the judge of the juvenile court in Indianapolis claimed that only 10 percent of the children placed on probation had committed a second offense, a 90 percent success rate.[2] In 1905, Judge Lindsey—who outdid so many people in so many ways— declared his opinion that there had been a substantial decrease in the number of serious offenses committed in every city in which the juvenile court had operated for any length of time; for his own city, Denver, he claimed a 95 percent success rate with children placed on probation.[3]

While measurements of the success of the juvenile court in terms of recidivism rates continued, they rapidly were overshadowed by a new vocabulary of evaluation which concentrated on the more indirect measure of the inventory of facilities available in juvenile courts for the rehabilitation of delinquents. Perhaps because of the difficulty of learning the facts concerning recidivism (accompanied perhaps by the fear of confronting the facts), by the end of the second decade of operation, the discourse began to focus heavily on the degree to which the real juvenile court approximated the ideal. Standards emerged for judging the courts which took with remarkable seriousness the rather vague promise of the founders that in the new era scientific study would uncover the causes and appropriate treatment of delinquency. Under the leadership of another progressive institution for the pursuit of child welfare—the United States Children's Bureau, created in 1912—the juvenile courts themselves came under careful scrutiny.

In 1918, the Children's Bureau conducted its first major survey of courts hearing children's cases. By this time, every state in the union but three had enacted juvenile court laws. The survey, conducted primarily by Evelina Belden, and published in 1920, distinguished between those courts which heard children's cases (over two thousand responded to the questionnaire) and those courts which were "specially organized" to hear children's cases. The minimal definition of specially organized courts included separate hearings for children, officially authorized probation service, and provision for recording social information and other data collected in the course of case investigations. By these standards, there were 321 specially organized courts in 1918. The definition of a true juvenile court went further: in addition to separate hearings, official probation, and recording of social data, the true juvenile court had informal or chancery courtroom procedure and provision for mental and physical examinations of children in connection with the court's decision-making process.[4] The survey ranged over all aspects of the treatment of juveniles from before their hearings through probation, concentrating on the separation from adult offenders, the quality of court-related personnel, and the nature of the contact between them and the children.

While most jurisdictions had complied with the first basic

standard of providing separate hearings for children, an alarming few had solved one of the problems that had most bothered juvenile court reformers—the pre-trial detention of children in jails where they mixed with adult offenders. Ten states reported not a single juvenile detention room or home. At least one court in each state sometimes used a jail for detention of children, often in violation of state law. Three hundred and seventy courts had no better provision for children detained for a hearing than a jail or almshouse. To be sure, the worst conditions prevailed in the more rural jurisdictions, where a much smaller proportion of the country's delinquents were handled than in the city, but even the urban courts, most of which had special detention rooms or homes at their disposal, sometimes detained children in jail.

This failure to comply with minimum standards for physical separation from adult offenders shocked many reformers. Katherine Lenroot, who had an outstanding career in government work on behalf of children, judged this failure harshly.

> Together with separate hearings and probation service, special detention facilities for children are a basic feature of juvenile court organization. In the absence of proper arrangements for detention, the original purpose of the juvenile court . . . must inevitably meet defeat in many cases.[5]

Of course, the goal of the juvenile court was not simply the separation of child from adult offender: the purpose of that separation, and of the court itself, was to make the legal process as it pertained to children constructive rather than merely punitive. In the short run, the juvenile court was intended to diagnose and treat individual delinquents; in the long run, the reformers hoped to discover scientific principles of behavior which would contribute to the prevention of delinquency. These goals depended on the collection of data about children who passed through the courts. The Children's Bureau Conference on Juvenile Court Standards in 1921 considered mental and physical examinations, both in service to individual delinquents and in pursuit of an understanding of the phenomenon of delinquency, to be an "essential" feature of a children's court.[6]

To meet the ideal of scientific treatment there appeared a series of court-affiliated clinics, staffed by physicians, psychologists, and social workers. The first of these opened under the direction of Dr. William Healy in Chicago in 1909. Dr. Healy, a student of William James and the teacher of a whole generation of social workers who became familiar through his works with a multifaceted, psychiatric approach to behavior problems, set a pattern for other early clinics by confining his focus at the Juvenile Psychopathic Institute to the problems of recidivists and "abnormals." The Chicago clinic, followed by similar institutions in Boston, Los Angeles, Detroit, New York, and Philadelphia, tried to administer a wide range of tests covering physical, social, and mental patterns in delinquent children. In 1921, the Commonwealth Fund undertook the creation of several demonstration clinics, and in this period such institutions began to serve not only the court but the entire community and to try to prevent as well as to cure delinquency. Unfortunately, the Commonwealth Fund experiment was allowed to expire, and the remaining fully staffed clinics did not come near to meeting the need for mental diagnosis in the juvenile courts.

In 1918, only thirteen courts, all in large cities, maintained clinics for court-related cases as part of the regular court organization. Only 145 courts, or 7 percent of those responding to the 1918 questionnaire, reported mental examinations for their clientele in clinics organized for that purpose or by trained persons with psychiatric or psychological knowledge. Another survey, published in 1928, showed that only 15 to 20 percent of the children whose cases were heard in courts that *did* have clinics available ever had psychological examinations, because the clinics could take only a few court cases a week. According to the survey's author, this meant that only 5 to 7 percent of the total juvenile court population had psychological diagnosis of an adequate sort.[7] Worse still, it was common for those courts that did give examinations to do so only for children who had already been committed to reformatories. To reserve mental examinations for such cases, and to reserve them until *after* such an important decision had been made, hardly fulfilled the ideal that all dispositions be based upon full knowledge of the child's circumstances and needs.

The courts more often provided physical check-ups, but like mental investigations, they often were given only on the eve of the child's entry into a reformatory and did not, therefore, contribute to the disposition of his case. Of those localities which did provide physical examinations as a part of their pre-disposition procedure, many gave them only to children who obviously suffered from some abnormal physical condition.

Although big city courts usually had better facilities than rural ones, a study of ten large cities conducted by the Children's Bureau in 1925 indicated that few even of their courts conducted a sufficiently thorough examination of children prior to disposition. The forms they used for the collection of social data were often superficial and unimaginative; investigators often did not bother to gather all the material requested on the forms; mental tests were usually confined to the determination of intelligence quotient. Three of these ten cities had no paid personnel capable of giving physical examinations, and consequently, only the occasional child with an obvious problem received one. The conclusion that "only one of the courts studied had provision for a well-rounded study of all important cases, including social, physical and mental factors" represented a serious indictment of a movement which should have been at its best-realized in such cities.

> Not only is scientific study indispensable to adequate understanding of individual children who come before the court, but unless the court knows the material with which it deals and the results of the treatment it prescribed it cannot measure its successes or failures.[8]

Scientific treatment of delinquency was not meant to be a luxury in juvenile court. Without universally available facilities for separate detention, and for physical and mental examinations, the juvenile court could not pretend to the scientific, rehabilitative ideal or fulfill the promise it had so optimistically made.

Given the importance of personal contact to the rehabilitative plan of the juvenile court, problems of facilities shaded quickly into problems of staff. An inadequate number of qualified and committed personnel, as much as the scarcity of detention homes and clinics, thwarted the ideal of scientific treatment. Indeed, for all their importance, facilities were not as important to the movement's supporters as were people. Reformers in the early movement believed that court workers "with the right vision and personality may achieve far more in the reconstruction of children than will a court with splendidly equipped quarters."9

Unfortunately, it soon became apparent that the juvenile court, even in its dewy-eyed first years, could only rarely draw to it the talent its architects felt necessary. Judges, for example, were reluctant to commit themselves to a lengthy stay in a position untested for its long-range effects on judicial careers.10 Further, juvenile court cases did not ordinarily seem as challenging as others. Consequently, despite years of propaganda celebrating the power and importance of the juvenile court judge and emphasizing the need for accumulated and continuous experience, judges were usually supplied by a system of rotation among men (and, occasionally, women) already assigned to other courts, with changes sometimes occurring as often as once every three months. In other jurisdictions the judge might be elected or appointed by the governor. None of these systems was ideal. While the rotation system discouraged expertness and commitment, election involved considerations irrelevant to the best interests of the court, and patronage appointments satisfied political purposes rather than the needs of the children for a talented staff.

The qualities of the judge in juvenile court were important because of the judge's potential for healing young lives, as supporters of the court emphasized, and because of his power to proceed without the usual constitutional restrictions, as the

occasional detractors of the court emphasized. He was important, too, because his attitude toward the philosophy of the
movement could determine, with far more certainty than any
legislation, whether indeed the ideal juvenile court would become a reality. By emphasizing speed and efficiency in the
disposition of cases, he might likewise dispose of the ideal of
careful, scientific, individualized treatment. By bending or
ignoring the probation system, he might use it in the service
of retributive justice. In 1906, the New York State Probation
Commission put the following question to a New York City
juvenile court judge and got the following answer:

> Question: Does the officer who visits the child's home be-
> come personally acquainted with the child?
> Answer: Not more than several contacts would bring; he
> would not endeavor to do more. I have not found it bene-
> ficial, where such an attempt has been made. . . . Some-
> times too much familiarity destroys control over the child. I
> think that fear is necessary in dealing with them, as well as
> the social meeting of them.[11]

In 1918, when there had been time for judges to adjust to the
juvenile court's philosophical orientation, the Belden survey
found that the reports of judges to the Children's Bureau
"frequently failed to . . . recognize the cardinal principle of
the juvenile court—that the purpose is not to punish but [to
provide] education and discipline suited to the needs of the
child. The terminology used in the replies frequently linked
the children with criminals."[12]

Although a full-time, long-range commitment on the part
of a judge to service in the juvenile court could not guarantee
that his service would be wise and just, it could at least make
more likely an attitude sympathetic to the philosophical ends
of the institution. Friends of the court therefore condemned
the rotation system and were dismayed by the findings of the
Belden survey: that in 1918 there were only twenty-three full-
time juvenile court judges in the entire country; that the
majority of children's judges spent a majority of their time on
other cases; that of the 321 courts which qualified as specially

organized to hear children's cases (16 percent of all those courts reporting children's cases), only thirty-one had judges who were specially assigned to the task. A few of these people became well known precisely for their devotion to the juvenile court. But the Ben Lindseys, people dedicated to unraveling the problem of delinquency from their position on the bench through warm personal relationships with delinquents, were rare indeed.

Along with the movement's emphasis on an informal rather than authoritarian approach to delinquents came the first definition of probation as a personal relationship, a friendship between the young delinquent and any "reputable person" who offered to do probation work. While luring the offender back to the straight and narrow, this friendship was also to bridge the gulf between the poor and the privileged. A gift of sympathy and individual contact was to replace the giving of alms. Hastings Hart, one of the drafters of Chicago's juvenile court law and, in 1906, the general superintendent of the Children's Home and Aid Society, reported that the early court advocates had believed that "any volunteer would answer as a probation officer."[13] At the very least, volunteers had the virtue of being expense-free and attracted to the work itself rather than to the monetary compensation. Indeed, to some reformers the use of volunteers was not simply a matter of convenience, for when faced with the inexorable advance of professional social work, they defended their preference for the amateur. They valued the spontaneity of the volunteer's work and feared that the trained would make the probation process less personal. They celebrated the worldly experience which the volunteer brought to his work, and compared it favorably to the mere book learning of professionals: the person who made a success in life would make the greatest success in probation work. The ideal qualities of a probation officer for the early juvenile court movement were sincerity, warmth, and tact.

It was not long, however, before social-service workers with professional yearnings found a role in the juvenile court movement and in the courts themselves. Before the end of the first

decade of the court's operation, the demand was growing for
paid probation service as the first line of attack on the problem
of delinquency.

Although expertise had an undeniable appeal to the progressive mind, its triumph in the juvenile court was assisted
by the fact that the volunteer system had quickly come to
seem inadequate. Among charity organization workers,
criticism of the amateur had begun as early as the 1890's; the
themes of the criticism—accusations of irregularity, in-
genuousness, inefficiency, and tendencies to moralize—
filtered into the juvenile court literature as friends of the court
came to distrust workers whose time was snatched from other
business and pleasures. In 1914, sociologist Thomas D. Eliot
declared that the volunteer probation system had already
proven a failure in twelve major cities,[14] and almost every
state which had probation service had responded by passing
legislation which permitted the appointment of paid personnel.

By the 1920's, the friendly volunteer was no longer the
model probation officer. The movement had by then embraced standards which included a thorough knowledge of
psychology and such qualities as efficiency, authority, and
skill. In 1923, Katherine Lenroot found that "professional
paid service is the only effective kind; volunteers must play
only a supplemental role."[15] Dr. William Healy, who exemplifies the new ideal of scientific as opposed to merely
affectional approaches to delinquency, wrote in 1926: "We are
not nowadays, at least very few of us, asking for any great
extension of sympathy for childhood, but we are asking for a
deeper and more extensive understanding of child life."[16]

Thus, by its own experience and by the pressure of the
emerging profession of social work, the juvenile court movement was converted to a new set of standards for the recruit-
ment and employment of probation officers: they had to be
full-time workers and receive compensation from public funds
in salaries competitive with those paid in other occupations;
they had to be selected on the basis of ability and training, and
not because they had political pull or good intentions. The

qualities of personality and character, which had alone de-fined the ideal probation officer in the early days, did not disappear altogether from the list of qualifications, but they tended to be less important as time went by.

The idea of the salaried, professional, full-time probation officer had been available as an alternative for at least a decade when the Belden survey was conducted in 1918. The survey, however, uncovered the fact that 55 percent of the courts hearing children's cases had no regular probation service at all; only eight states had a recognized probation officer for every court within its borders. And of the 45 percent which did have probation, fewer than half had regular officers giving full-time service paid for by the court. Even where the law provided for the appointment of paid personnel, the intent of the legislators could be and sometimes was subverted by the unwillingness of the judge to make the authorized appointments. Sometimes the creation of salaried positions served only to increase the possibilities for patronage gifts by local politicians. Indeed, some saw the desire of politicians for patronage jobs as the greatest threat of all to the proper development of probation work, and reformers repeatedly called for the control of these appointments either by civil-service examinations or state supervisory boards.

Nevertheless, the selection of probation officers remained in the hands of the judges. In 1925, nine of the ten large cities surveyed by the Children's Bureau left probation appointments to the judge. In only three cities of the ten were appointments made on the basis of competitive examinations, and at most, performance on such exams was weighed as only 50 percent of the consideration for selection. These methods combined with inadequate salaries produced a staff with little formal preparation and almost no previous experience.

Finally, the inadequate size of staffs in those courts which did have probation service produced yet another cause for criticism. Although the Conference on Juvenile Court Standards in 1921 agreed that the maximum number of cases which a probation officer could carry conscientiously was fifty, in the ten cities of the Lenroot survey the average number of cases per officer ran from 36 to 156. Three of these cities assigned averages of well over a hundred cases to each of their officers; only three assigned case loads which consistently fell within the advised maximum. It seemed that even in those relatively few courts with regular probation service, treatment was likely to be superficial because of overwhelming case loads.

With the change from volunteer to paid personnel came increasing emphasis on the constructive possibilities of probation work. Probation was more than a humane substitute for imprisonment, more than "another chance," and more than mere supervision for the purpose of preventing new infractions of the law. Probation was intended to reform the child, to elevate him, and to help him fulfill his human potentialities. In order to achieve those goals, the probation officer had, at the very least, to have continuing knowledge of the child and his daily life.

In order to stay in touch with his charges, the probation officer usually required them to report to the probation office at regular intervals, either individually or as a group. On such occasions the children would bring written accounts of their performance at school or at work, spend a few minutes with the officer, and then depart. In some courts the judge used these gatherings of probationers as an opportunity to deliver a little lecture and to make a cursory survey of their progress. Visits of probationers to the ten courts studied by Lenroot and Lundberg took place with a frequency of once a week to once a month. In two courts all the probationers met together with the judge; in eight courts there were confidential interviews of about five minutes each, ten minutes for serious cases. The manual for New York State probation officers defended court visits as a means of teaching "punctuality and obedience to law and authority,"[17] but the possibility for constructive work in the rushed, harried atmosphere of the probation office seemed rather slim. Further, by bringing each delinquent child into regular contact with other delinquent children, court visits threatened to reinforce antisocial patterns as reformatory institutions had.

Even at best, such court appearances were no substitute for visits to the children's homes by probation officers. Because delinquency seemed to result from negative influences in the environment, probation was no treatment at all if it failed to deal with the child's surroundings. The Children's Bureau Committee on Juvenile Court Standards in 1921 decided that home visits at least once every two weeks, except in rare cases, were necessary even for merely adequate probation work. Other theorists recommended regular weekly visits, and in difficult cases more.

Home visits, the essence of the treatment which was in turn the essence of the juvenile court, obviously did not take place at all in the many jurisdictions which had no probation service. In many medium-sized cities the courts scheduled home visits haphazardly. Of the ten large cities in the Lenroot survey, five had courts which scheduled home visits less than once a month to each child; two achieved rates of only one visit every two months, or one every three months in less serious cases. Even in the best-developed court systems, probation officers saw far less of their charges than the theorists thought necessary.

The amount of attention given probationers was only one determinant of the quality of probation work. The Belden survey indicated that at least in those jurisdictions which used police personnel in the probation department not only the amount of time accorded each child but the spirit in which it was accorded fell far short of the ideal.

> It was evident from the character of the replies of many of the police probation officers that they considered their duties in connection with children to be limited to conveying a child to an institution or jail, arresting or swearing out a petition against him, or presenting evidence in court. The constructive side of casework for children under their supervision did not appear in many of their reports.[18]

Similarly discouraging was the evidence collected by the Lenroot survey.

Only in a surprisingly few instances was an understanding of
the meaning and spirit of probation given the child. . . .
The definite terms of probation were over-emphasized and
the conditions of probation were too negative and prohibi-
tory.[19]

Six of the ten courts left the terms of probation to the officers
to decide; five courts distributed printed statements of the
conditions of probation, making no pretense to individualized
dispositions. The staffs received little supervision and gave
little conscious and coherent consideration to their task. Probation systems were characterized by "uneven work, uncertain
policies, unnecessarily prolonged probation periods, and often
friction within the staff."[20] Another effort to ascertain the
real quality of probation work uncovered shocking mishan-
dling of the system, especially in Cincinnati, where the court
had no record of some of the cases on probation, no one knew
how many cases were still active, and no one had given any
attention at all to some probationers for eighteen months; the
staff had simply lost track of many others.[21]

It became almost comfortable, in the face of such revelations, to conclude that probation had never really been tried
and therefore could not be judged. Many courts did not even
attempt to ascertain the results of their own work, but in spite
of the difficulties in measuring the results of rehabilitative
efforts, by the 1920's some commentators were trying to decide just how effective the system had been and were dis-
covering genuine malfunction.

The Lenroot survey pieced together the records of three
courts over a five-year period. It reported that respectively 25,
31, and 39 percent of the children placed on probation by
these courts were subsequently committed for failing on probation or for some new delinquency within five years of their
initial appearance in court. A much more thorough study
made by Dr. Healy and Augusta Bronner in 1926 revealed
that 50 percent of the children who had passed through the
Chicago juvenile court between 1909 and 1914 had adult
court records and 37 percent had been committed to adult
correctional institutions.[22]

In the 1930's, the inquiry into recidivism rates continued. A monograph on probation published in 1934 concluded that probation had achieved a remarkable degree of success, but the evidence which it cited was at best equivocal: after a period of five to seven years from the first appearance in court, 43 percent of the boys were considered "permanent successes"; 34 percent had been dismissed from probation but had returned to the court for new offenses, and these were called "temporary successes"; 21 percent had been declared failures while still under the jurisdiction of the court; and 2 percent were undetermined. The "remarkable degree of success" then, consisted of 43 percent rehabilitated and 55 percent persisting in delinquency. The records of children while they were still on probation were even worse: 61 percent of the children on probation returned to court during their first month for violation of probation or for some other delinquency.[23] Sheldon and Eleanor Glueck's 1934 study, *One Thousand Delinquents*, examined the conduct of delinquent boys during the five years following their treatment in juvenile court. They concluded that "88% of them continued their delinquencies during this period. They were arrested on the average of 3.6 times each, nor were the arrests of our youths essentially for petty offenses. . . . The major conclusion is inescapable, then, that the treatment carried out by clinic, court and associated community facilities had very little effect in preventing recidivism."[24] Healy and Bronner confirmed these results in 1935, and found in addition that the record of recidivism was worse for the period 1924–25 than for the period 1917–22.[25]

It was inevitable that the many evaluations of juvenile court facilities and success rates would affect opinion both inside the juvenile court and in related professions. By the 1920's, many juvenile courts handled more than half their cases without benefit of judge or formal inquiry, and some treated 75 to 95 percent of their cases this way.[26] Court workers advocated unofficial disposition of cases not only to relieve the overworked court machinery but to spare the child the stigma of a court record.[27] This increase in unofficial treatment was a confession that the juvenile court had not succeeded in convincing the public that its adjudications of delinquency were any less damning than criminal convictions. But more than that, it was a tacit admission that the courtroom experience, once conceived as a constructive step toward the rehabilitation of young offenders, no longer represented part of the treatment but seemed more to be part of the disease, to be encountered only at the risk of contamination. After all the discussions of chancery origins, chancery procedure seemed a stranger in many juvenile courts. Five of the big city courts which Lenroot and Lundberg surveyed in 1925 claimed to have chancery procedure, but the researchers found that the atmosphere in the courtrooms varied widely from the spirit reformers associated with that procedure; in almost half of these ten urban courts, they found that the conduct of hearings was "quasi-criminal." In 1929, J. Prentice Murphy wrote an article entitled "The Juvenile Court at the Bar: A National Challenge," in which he concluded that the notion of juvenile courts as "separate and distinct from the spirit and practice of the criminal courts . . . with certain exceptions . . . [was] an observation at absolute variance with the facts."[28]

While they tried to adjust to these disquieting reports, court supporters in the twenties looked back on their predecessors and condemned them for having made exaggerated claims, for "having stupidly vaunted themselves" in their role as reformers.[29] By contrast, the younger generation observed in itself a "queer current of dissatisfaction" with the quality of its work.[30] They watched uneasily as the "swelling tide of disrepute threatened to engulf much of the social work . . . for delinquents."[31]

Just as doubts about the constructive nature of the courtroom experience had led workers to advocate diversion from formal hearings, doubts about the efficacy of rehabilitative efforts suggested that the courts were perhaps making the mistake of putting too many children on probation. Both for the good of the child, who got too little attention from overworked probation officers, and for the good of the community, which had the right to protection from more serious delinquents, the public demanded greater caution than the courts were demonstrating in the use of probation.[32] From within the probation establishment came charges that were more embarrassing. The New York field secretary of the National Probation Association told the National Conference of Social Work in 1926 that the staff in whose hands the probation system rested included far too many "political hangers-on" and "untrained, uneducated weaklings."[33] More soberly, a self-styled friend of the probation system and prominent professor of social work wrote in 1923 that the probation system, like the procedure of the juvenile court, had not traveled far enough from the system which it had been intended to replace.

> Some years ago I expressed myself to the effect that probation offered more toward the reconstruction of the offender than any other process of the criminal law, and I see no reason for changing the opinion then expressed. But in common with other friends of probation I am deeply concerned over the fact that this process is becoming increasingly identified with the older traditional processes of the criminal law, instead, as we had hoped, of cultivating a trend which is distinctly in the opposite direction.[34]

The personnel of the juvenile court and social work movements began themselves to find fault with every conceivable aspect of the court enterprise. What could be the result of such an ill-equipped, poorly supervised, inefficient, and philosophically backward effort?

Some researchers in the twenties continued to maintain that the evidence was insufficient, but few gave the court's supporters much encouragement. One study concluded in 1928 that there was no correlation between court procedure and success in rehabilitation, which indicated that at best the court's architects had been confused.[35] In his characteristically moderate voice, Dr. William Healy said that the extent to which "the juvenile court system is effective is an open question. We are making some studies which do not seem to prove by any manner of means that the juvenile court alone or the probation system alone is turning the boy from delinquency."[36]

Other voices were more severe. They stated unequivocally that the juvenile court wasn't working. Not outsiders who were impatient to see some results from an institution they distrusted, but insiders who were in deep sympathy with the court's intentions, they found that the courts had not succeeded in preventing further delinquency in the children they "treated"; recidivism persisted. At best, the juvenile courts were holding their own against crime, but a holding action was far less than the reformers had hoped for. The judge of the Los Angeles juvenile court thought in 1924 that it was far from enough.

> If after all these years of development and extension of corrective principles and work of the juvenile courts and of the schools and agencies with which the wards of those courts are placed; if after all the years of effort in the field of welfare work by the many societies outside those courts; if after all of that, we are holding our own, then those efforts must be multiplied indefinitely or the plan of attack radically changed, if we are to make any real headway.[37]

Such gloominess about the quality of treatment in the juvenile court released resentment against its legal peculiarities. It became increasingly difficult to skirt the question of whether the treatment offered by the juvenile court justified the abandonment of procedural safeguards. Judge Julian Mack had warned in 1909 concerning incarceration of juveniles that the truth that a reformatory was a prison, "in the enthusiasm of the juvenile court movement, is in danger of being overlooked. If a child must be taken away from its home, if for the natural parental care that of the state is to be substituted, a real school, not a prison in disguise, must be provided."[38] A few others had issued similar warnings in the relatively early days, usually focusing in particular on the dangers of incarceration. As the practical failings of the juvenile court became more apparent, concern about the power of the juvenile court over the child became more general and

widespread. Especially in view of the primitive state of knowledge concerning the proper mode of treatment for delinquency, growing numbers of writers warned of the dangers
inherent in the system.

In the cheerful early days, only the rare skeptic pondered
the possibility that the juvenile court would be unable to provide the kind of treatment which would warrant the suspen-
sion of procedural safeguards. Rather, it was assumed that the
rehabilitative ideal would be reached as soon as the shackles
of legal formality had cleared the way for scientific treatment.
But after years of struggling to realize their correctional utopia,
and reams of external and internal criticism, it seemed that
there might indeed have been something lost, in exchange for
which not quite enough had been gained. In 1923, the
Children's Bureau Committee on Juvenile Court Standards
wondered whether when a child's freedom and reputation
were at stake, he didn't have a right to due process of law.[39]

Still, the "queer current of doubt" about the quality of
work in the juvenile court ran through a fundamental conviction that the court as it had been originally designed had come
to stay. It was neither a general failure nor a universal success.
It was not a panacea, but it was not a mistake, either. The
application of the early reformers' principles, not the principles themselves, had come into question.

The juvenile court movement had gained easy acceptance
of its ideas but met disappointment and frustration in convert-
ing those ideas into reality. The programs that had seemed so
rational and promising in the abstract encountered in the first
twenty or thirty years what must have seemed an endless
parade of difficulties, which proceeded not so much from the
expected quarters of reluctant legislatures and hidebound
courts of review as from within the institution itself.

Discouraging as it was, however, the painful comparison of
the real with the ideal would not necessarily have doomed the
juvenile court movement. Of equal consequence to the court's
future was the activity at its fringes in the related fields of
psychology and sociology, where a conceptual reorientation
was undermining assumptions about the nature of child and

man. As positivist criminology divided into psychological and cultural theories concerning the genesis of crime, and as each division elaborated its insights, it became apparent that the model of the criminal as constrained could have discouraging implications for institutions built on the rehabilitative ideal.

5
PSYCHOLOGY

When the juvenile court was first created, Joseph Hawes suggests, the social sciences were insufficiently developed to help the court do the job of individualized justice. Hawes believes that insofar as there existed in the late nineteenth century a core of professional theorists and practitioners in the field of criminal behavior, it was made up largely of prison physicians and criminal anthropologists who presented a far more pessimistic picture of the possibilities for rehabilitation than did the juvenile court reformers. Whether, if the social sciences had already been better developed and had retained this pessimistic stance, the juvenile court reformers would have found some accommodation with them is, of course, not knowable. The point is that the relative underdevelopment of the professional social sciences left the reformers free to apply their own notions of child development and antisocial behavior. In particular, while the juvenile court "seemed to be an ideal vehicle for the application of the teachings of social science to America's troubled youth,"[1] it was in fact in its early life largely a vehicle for the moralism and exaggerated hopes of amateurs.

The reformers did, nevertheless, by their concentration on constructive treatment based on individual circumstances and their analogies with medicine, invite the participation of social scientists in the theory and practice of juvenile justice. Hawes may exaggerate by saying that when the invitation was taken up the juvenile court reformers regarded the social scientists with "dismay" because their message indicated that reform was a "waste of time,"[2] but it is true that in the last half century the insights of the social sciences have made the premises of the juvenile court seem at best hopelessly naïve.

The intellectual and social foundations of the movement began to shift in the twenties, and the institution which had been touted precisely because it had taken its cue from up-to-the-minute notions became increasingly outdated. Some of the court's adherents tried to shore it up with modern underpinnings, but no such efforts could curb the tendency of a growing number of writers to experiment with psychological and sociological theories which threatened the court's rationale.

The juvenile court movement's commitment to individualized treatment opened the door to an eventual shift from the volunteer probation staff to a paid and trained one. As the twentieth century grew older, the field of social work grew alongside the juvenile court and social workers exerted increasing influence on the court. As others have pointed out, the first effect of this contact may well have been to reinforce the faith that the reformers could indeed achieve their aim: professional social adjusters do, of course, have a vested interest in believing that social adjustment is possible.[3] But the orientation toward human behavior which social work eventually adopted may nevertheless have undermined the apparent efficacy of the juvenile court.

Social work was born peacefully and quietly from the tradition of charity. The first corps of proto-social workers was the group of women who undertook in the late nineteenth century the task of "friendly visiting" among the poor, with a view to effecting their moral, spiritual, and economic uplift (in that order). The dominant concern of this embryonic social work was correction.

While friendly visiting no doubt derived in part from motives of genuine good will and a desire to share and to alleviate the conditions of the poor, the sick, and the criminal, it held up a standard of propriety which the socially deprived were expected to meet in exchange for assistance. Whatever the relationship between visitor and client, it did not rest on an assumption of equality. Roy Lubove writes in his history of social work:

> The relationship between visitor and client may have been personal, but it was not "friendly" in the sense of the informal, natural cohesiveness of peers. . . . The visitor saw in her client less an equal or potential equal than an object of charitable reform whose unfortunate and lowly condition resulted from ignorance or deviations from middle-class values and patterns of life-organization. . . .[4]

While on the surface the friendly visitor considered her clients as wayward children in need of guidance toward the Right Way, another sentiment—more obscure and less willingly confessed—often ran below the surface: the apprehension of what might develop if the poor were left to themselves. The Fifth Annual Report of the Charities Organization Society of New York warned in 1887: "If we do not furnish the poor with elevating influences, they will rule us with degrading ones."[5]

Early volunteer court workers often shared this attitude, which aimed not only at helping others but also at preserving their own middle-class ways. As Anthony Platt points out, the language they used in their child-saving work—words like " 'purity,' 'salvation,' 'innocence,' 'corruption' "—indicated their faith in the "righteousness" of their cause.[6] It also indicated that to a large extent the tools they had for dealing with social problems were the tools of conventional morality and popularized Christian virtue.

But if these proto-social workers looked backward to a moral solution to social problems, they also helped open the way to a less judgmental and more "scientific" approach. There was emerging at the turn of the century an inclination to regard deviance as the result of the economic and social conditions of poverty, and to regard poverty less as a matter of individual guilt than of social malfunction. This focus on social and economic conditions suggested a particular approach to treatment: the surrounding environment and the forces at work on individual conduct, including other human beings, needed attention at least as much as did the individual client himself. Although the rhetoric referred to individualized treatment, it meant treatment of a collective case, not necessarily of an individual client. The focus of this approach settled upon the family.

The culmination of this concept of treatment came in 1917 with the publication of social work's first full-length quasi-scientific statement of the theory and practice of casework—Mary Richmond's *Social Diagnosis*. Miss Richmond's book contributed to casework the concept of the social self: the individual was defined and could only be understood by his relations with other human beings. Accordingly, the data upon which the worker based diagnosis and treatment consisted largely in the testimony of the client's friends and relatives, not in firsthand contact with the client himself.

Though Miss Richmond's ideas were popular and influential, the participation of the United States in World War I turned social work in another direction—toward a much greater dependency on psychiatric techniques and consequently toward a greater emphasis on the client's inner, rather than his social, life.[7] In part the shift was due to the multitude of new patients who appeared as an unanticipated by-product of the war and who, having no history of dependency or other social malfunction, seemed to present problems of a uniquely emotional nature and thus to demand a different response, one that focused on the independent personality.[8]

After the war the preeminence in social work of the individual client continued undiminished. By 1920, the profession was committed to a view of behavior which put mental content at the center and pointed to a psychological approach to behavior problems. Among the elements of the new approach was an effort to remove the tone of moral superiority from the caseworker's relationship to his client. Some of the attempts were awkward and superficial, such as Edward Devine's discussion in 1922 of "social work" as an appropriate name for the profession.

It is at least preferable to the clumsy "social welfare work" and to "social service" since the sturdy Anglo-Saxon "work" carries no suggestion of the class distinctions associated with "service" and "uplift work," which is even more obviously objectionable for the same reason. . . .[9]

Though not immune to the temptations of class and ethnic superiority, Devine was clearly bending his energies toward minimizing the paternalistic tone of social work.

In more sophisticated hands this reorientation took the form, in the late twenties and thirties, of an effort to eliminate moral judgments from social work altogether. Social workers gradually came to regard behavior as a psychological rather than a moral phenomenon, and agreed that "to change it [behavior] is a scientific rather than a moral problem."[10] In 1929, a book on the relation of psychology to social work declared that "one of the outstanding revelations of modern science is that the implications of misconduct are frequently more pathological than moral."[11] The avowed purpose in investigating a client's background no longer lay in a desire to judge where he had been right and where wrong, but simply in a desire to elucidate and explain his behavior. The authors wrote:

Such data are secured not for the purpose of furnishing the basis of an ethical judgment of the client, but for the scientific purpose of determining the cause of his predicament. . . . Only recently have we come to realize that behavior which is wholly immoral from a superficial point of view may be entirely pathological in its significance and due to factors which have no moral implications whatever.[12]

Though they may have found it difficult in practice, social workers tried to persuade each other to make a break with the moralistic past and embrace the scientific future.

In this mood, social workers changed the primary aim of their endeavors from charity and correction to adjustment. In 1925, Miriam Van Waters, then the able and energetic referee of the Los Angeles juvenile court and participant in many local and national efforts to improve the treatment of criminals, believed that the task of social work was to use the "tools of science and business to bring about adjustments which are necessary between the individual and his human world for successful living together."[13] It followed that the social worker was no longer to pity his clients or to call upon them for repentance. The practitioner did not have to bring his client into conformity with a model of social perfection: he had to consider the preservation of the individual as well as the preservation of the social order.

While the new definition of social work made less constrictive demands upon clients, it nevertheless complicated the relationship between the client and the social worker. The emphasis on adjustment required that social workers abandon the comfortable techniques of exhortation and good example and enter the unfamiliar realm of therapy. Virginia Robinson, a social worker who was more passionately committed than most to psychiatric social work, suggested that the traditional preoccupation with collecting and analyzing data had all along been a device for avoiding the basic responsibility of administering real treatment. Now, however, social workers had come to see that the client needed a good deal more than friendship: he needed trained and disciplined assistance. The nature of that assistance, regardless of the patient's particular problem, would involve the use of psychiatric techniques by a professional social worker.

These trends in the method and content of social work touched the juvenile court directly. The notion that therapy, not friendship, was the essential ingredient in the proper relationship between social worker and client demanded much more thorough, prolonged, and frequent contact between client and worker than the probation system had promised or provided. The superficial and essentially disciplinary relationship between probation officer and delinquent could only seem inadequate in the light of new social-work standards: not only did the program in practice fall short of its original conception, but even its ideal formulation seemed ill suited to the task of social readjustment. The early penchant of the juvenile court for unpaid volunteer probation officers and of charity organizations for friendly visitors had been no coincidence: they were two strands of the same thread. In the teens, the rather smooth and brisk transition to paid probation officers in juvenile court professionalized the staff but did not necessarily change the relationship between officer and probationer. The shift to a psychological focus in social work brought with it a demand for a parallel shift in the juvenile court movement, not the least because the personnel of the two movements overlapped. The commitment of social workers to a psychological approach affected the juvenile court the more profoundly because of the kind of psychology it eventually brought to the task of rehabilitation.

Psychology's first penetration of the practices of American social work and crime prevention came in the decade of the teens, when workers in both fields had a serious and prolonged flirtation with the techniques of mental testing.

In 1905 Alfred Binet introduced his standards for the measurement of intelligence. Immediately the scientific-minded welcomed his method of quantification, and the intelligence quotient began its over-long history as a vital statistic. For years intelligence testing took the lead as the favorite tool of social diagnosis.

> In the decade . . . 1910–20, the intellectual factor and its importance in determining individual differences and behavior was exaggerated. . . . It was seized upon by groups of workers who were balked by behavior problems, chiefly in the courts, and in feeble-minded, penal, and reformatory institutions.[14]

The emergence and spread of the mental-defect theory of misconduct was a threat to the juvenile court, not because of its particular analysis of behavior, but because of its underlying assumption and implication: that the source of antisocial activity lay in unmodifiable and perhaps hereditary conditions. This assumption was of course being made by eugenicist contemporaries of the juvenile court reformers. But mental testing brought it into the juvenile court, from which it had previously been largely absent. Such pessimism was inimical to the very idea of the juvenile court, which rested on the notion that antisocial behavior could be modified. The suggestion that modification was impossible or even extremely difficult helped undermine the reformers' fundamental optimism.

Nevertheless, juvenile court workers and others concerned with crime and delinquency temporarily embraced mental testing as the key to their puzzle. While no one thought that mental deficiency accounted for 100 percent of delinquency cases, many students of deviance devoted 100 percent of their time to discussing and experimenting with mental testing. The extent of the fad was revealed in the *Journal of Delinquency,* a publication ostensibly dedicated to exploration of all aspects of the delinquency problem, which during these years included almost nothing but articles relating to testing techniques and intelligence as a determinant of behavior.

Researchers offered the mental-defect theory with endless variations. Estimates of the extent of feeblemindedness in the delinquent population varied widely, ranging between 25 and 75 percent, depending upon the category of offenders under discussion and the discussant. Some thought that feeblemindedness operated directly by preventing the child from understanding, and therefore from obeying, social rules. According to this view, the large proportion of wrongdoers was likely to come from low-intelligence groups, "for the simple reason that these children have not sufficient intelligence either to understand the laws or to adapt themselves to them."[15] Others thought that mental deficiency worked indirectly on children to twist their behavior.

> Mental subnormality . . . low mental age is a large inducement to, not a cause of, crime. . . . It means not that mentally subnormal individuals are destined to a criminal career, but that it is far easier for such individuals to be led into temptation.[16]

By making a child unsuccessful in school, mental deficiency increased his susceptibility to the forces that created criminals.

While the mental-deficiency theory of crime enjoyed a great vogue during the teens and persisted into the twenties, the composite portrait of the delinquent did not invariably include mental deficiency. Most writers continued to give major importance to environmental factors. Nevertheless, the flirtation of psychologists, social workers, and criminologists with intelligence testing introduced some crucial concepts into the juvenile court movement. First, it injected a note of pessimism into prevailing attitudes toward the socially maladjusted. Second, it suggested that experience and environmental conditions were not direct determinants of behavior but were important only as they filtered through a particular mental apparatus; it suggested that the final arbiter of the meaning of any experience was not the outside world but the inner one, and that the individual consciousness rather than social causes molded behavior. Thus, it focused attention on the individual, making social histories less relevant in at least one class of social-work cases.

The mental-testing approach to diagnosis was soon discredited, primarily by studies that pointed to a high incidence of mental deficiency in the socially adjusted portion of the population. By showing that many people sustained an acceptable relationship with society in spite of low intelligence, these studies helped convince social workers that mental incapacity alone could be considered a direct cause of maladjustment only in a limited number of cases. But the psychological, individual orientation introduced by the mental-defect theory became a lasting part of the social-work approach and received reinforcement from other developments in psychiatry.

With the end of the intelligence-testing craze came a redefinition of the role and scope of psychology. Just as history embraces and pulls together all elements of collective human life, so psychology began to include and interrelate all the elements in the life of the individual. Dr. Bernard Glueck of the New York School of Social Work wrote in 1923:

> There was a time . . . when the contributions of psychology and psychiatry were conceived to be limited to the task of defining whether a given delinquent was feeble-minded or insane. . . .
>
> Now, in actual practice, in . . . any sphere of human endeavor, psychiatry has come to define its task as that of understanding and treatment of human behavior.[17]

When the Children's Bureau in the early 1920's suggested the necessity of a mental examination for all children brought to the attention of legal authorities, mental examinations no longer meant simply intelligence tests; those efforts at quantification now provided only one part of the information needed about a child's mental life. Decrying past overemphasis on the matter of intelligence, many writers called upon their social-work colleagues to recognize and practice a more inclusive sort of psychology. The aim was to discover the general mental framework with which clients organized their experience.

One indication of the tendency to locate the proximal source of behavior in the mind and to broaden the definition of mental life was a new flexibility in discussing the causes of crime. Perhaps the first signs of response in the field of delinquency came in the form of a reluctance to talk about any one or two causes of crime as primary. Though widely touted as a new approach and though more sophisticated than the one-cause theories, this formulation was no more than a variation on the positivist theme. In fact, the picture of the delinquent as propelled by a multiplicity of forces did not differ significantly from the picture of the delinquent propelled by one force: he was still constrained and not personally responsible for his acts. The multicause theory did, however, permit greater flexibility in diagnosis and rested on the notion that it was not so much experience as the perception of it that determined behavior.

The idea that criminal behavior originated in individual perception of reality and not in objective reality itself did not emerge from theoretical ruminations alone. Much to the frustration of the experts, experience had indicated for years that the efforts to pinpoint causes in the environment and in physical conditions were hopeless. Dr. F. H. Allen, director of the Philadelphia Child Guidance Clinic, wrote in 1923: "The delinquent acts of juveniles show . . . striking uniformity and yet how diverse are the personalities and backgrounds and the individual experience that are back of this behavior."[18] Dr. William Healy, who had raised one of the few cautioning voices during the mental-testing craze, finally had an appreciative audience. He pointed out in 1923 how frequently people defied any and all supposed causes of delinquency and lived peacefully in society.

> We must not become cranks and account for too much of the trouble by some theory, for one time we were all much taken with the adenoid theory, and another time with the defective eyesight theory; another time much delinquency was due to congenital syphilis. But then we find that there are many individuals who have very bad posture and adenoids, who have been victims of congenital disease, but who have still not developed bad conduct.[19]

One by one he eliminated the social situations usually called upon to explain the origins of antisocial acts. According to his analysis of thousands of cases, success or failure in the rehabilitation of delinquents showed no significant correlation with poverty, broken homes, physical or mental defects, or nationality.[20] Dr. William A. White had reached a similar conclusion in 1920:

> A great mass of evidence shows that serious breaks in adjustment do not ordinarily occur without the cooperation of some lack of balance in the personality makeup, that they are rarely to be satisfactorily accounted for by the influence of extraneous circumstances alone. The studies of delinquents show this very well.[21]

Even people who had participated in the juvenile court movement from its inception felt the change. In 1942, Henry Thurston, once Chicago's chief juvenile probation officer, looked back over his career and wrote: "In 1905 no one of us had more than an inkling of the complex causes of delinquency."[22] Each time someone looked carefully at the statistics, he was struck by the blunt refusal of people to follow the predictions of criminologists.

Soon the experience of inaccurate predictions and the influence of a growing preoccupation with emotional and personality problems fused to produce a thoroughly individualistic theory of antisocial behavior.

This shift in the understanding of social problems disrupted the patterns both of probation work and of social work in general. When causes had seemed simply and directly environmental, the caseworker or probation officer contented himself with superficial adjustments in the exterior life of the child—securing a job, finding a foster home, enforcing school attendance. When the causes had seemed to involve mental ability, the job of the probation officer was even less difficult. Dealing with the feebleminded involved very little probing; measures for dealing with defectives—segregation or sterilization—were not the domain of the social worker, and therefore the intelligence-testing fad had the result of separating diagnosis and treatment. Since the solution for both environmental and hereditary problems seemed less complex than the diagnosis, concentration had naturally focused on the latter. However, once social workers began to see the causes of social problems as interior to the client, two changes followed: first, the raw material for diagnosis had to come primarily from the client, not from his friends and relatives; and second, the process of extracting this data from the client tended to merge with the process of effecting an adjustment, so that the differences between diagnosis and treatment faded and the importance of treatment, in the context of a truly individualistic psychology, began to match if not surpass the importance of diagnosis.

This change again complicated the task of the caseworker. Now diagnosis involved more than filling out a social-history form and administering an intelligence test. After a more probing and sophisticated diagnosis, something equally sophisticated in the way of treatment had to follow. Dr. Healy and

Augusta Bronner came to believe that "clinical diagnostic service is not of itself therapeutic" and was therefore not adequate.[23] Dr. Bernard Glueck thought that "back of these perverted behavior expressions lie causes that rightly call for the attention of the psychiatrist."[24] From friendly visitor to psychiatrist—the price of the psychological approach to behavior was the necessity of meeting much higher standards for work in modifying behavior.

In sum, the changes that occurred in the content of social work during and after World War I made new and serious demands on the juvenile court if it wished to retain status as a social and not merely a legal institution. Old methods seemed obsolete: the skills required to fill out a life-history form would never meet the challenge of exploring the personality of a child; the good will required to visit a probationer in the slums would never suffice in the art of therapy; the data so easily collected by means of prodding and poking and measuring in a clinic would not reveal the remote, unconscious workings of the delinquent's mind. The problem was no longer on the surface; now the juvenile court would have to dig for it and its solution.

The rise of professional psychology in any form might have required the juvenile court to reevaluate its ways or to prepare to defend itself. But the particular forms that psychological theory took in the twenties and thereafter implied serious challenges to the court idea. In the teens and twenties, two major interpretations of human behavior emerged as rivals for the allegiance of students and healers of men. The first was John Watson's behaviorism, which enjoyed something of a rebirth in the 1960's, and the second was, of course, the psychoanalytic theory of Sigmund Freud.

Watson offered America a short cut to behavior reform. By ignoring mental dimensions and emphasizing the Pavlovian phenomenon of conditioning and reconditioning, behaviorism kept all the variables in view and within control. Behavior was the result of stimulus-response conditioning, and the modification of behavior was a matter of reconditioning.

Watson's clear-cut mechanistic approach did not appeal to

practitioners in this country. Although habit clinics arose to deal with the problems of children, they never really took root. Virginia Robinson, scornful of all but psychiatric techniques, explained the cool response to behaviorism among social workers as follows:

> Alluring as the behavioristic approach may be in its offer of objective measures, definite procedures, and more assured controls, it fails for these very reasons to satisfy the needs of the case worker confronted with the problem of understanding a deep-laid pattern of emotional response and guiding a process in which her own patterns of interacting play a constant part.[25]

This statement illustrated at the same time it explained reservations about behaviorism, for it missed the point when it referred to "deep-laid pattern of emotional response." The very message of behaviorism suggested that one need not bother with remote considerations in order to understand and change behavior; such patterns, if they existed, were inaccessible to the scientist and irrelevant to remedial work. But Watson's message fell on deaf or distracted ears, for few social workers or probation officers were ready to believe that the matter was so simple. They felt that behaviorism ignored important facts of psychological life. Dr. Samuel Kohs, executive director of the Federation of Jewish Charities, explained in 1929:

> Behaviorism's . . . outspoken or tacit negation of consciousness, of will, judgment, the capacity of introspection, and its value for the understanding of others and of self, are definitely disadvantages in the effort to develop well-rounded point of view and technique in modifying human conduct.[26]

Behaviorism offered a great deal in the way of structured objectivity and scientific-sounding techniques, but in the end it seemed to social workers that for these very reasons it was superficial and flawed. In a contest with the more impressionistic approach of the Freudian school it could not prevail. Kohs made the comparison between behaviorism and psychiatry:

> On the one hand the former maintains that only those manifestations of human mental functioning which can be tested or smelled, weighed or measured, or have some form of objective reality, only those categories are really the subject matter of scientific psychology. The latter, on the other hand, contends that there are certain intangible and as yet immeasurable realities which cannot be left out of account. . . . The objectivist (or behaviorist) is inclined to minimize the significance of such psychological categories as conscience, the moral self, will, and similar mental manifestations which have a very direct and vital bearing on human conduct.[27]

Perhaps because they were reluctant to part entirely with the psychological categories of conscience, reason, and will; perhaps because they sought a system of prevention as well as a cure, people involved in social work and its allied activities rejected the bright-and-shining simplicity of behaviorism and elected the darker, more mysterious view of man embodied in Freudian psychology.

Freud's famous visit to Clark University in 1909 introduced his ideas to the American public. For the first years after the visit his ideas spread slowly and reached only a few corners of the professional population: the progressive era in America did not afford much growing room to theories like psychoanalysis. Only with the beginning of World War I did the lay public meet Freudian theory in its periodicals, and the versions that appeared deleted sexual references.

During the war, however, Freudian theory gradually emerged in unexpurgated form and began its conquest of America. Discussion of sex no longer met with much resistance, and indeed, in some quarters, one's social success depended on making sex a normal part of conversation. In some circles it was a mark of one's sophistication as well to be able to discuss one's own psychoanalysis or to "psychoanalyze" a friend. Floyd Dell and his companions in the literarty set which congregated in Greenwich Village in the second decade

of the twentieth century went about "psyching" each other
and the people they passed in the street. Psychoanalysis became a form of small talk. As Sherwood Anderson reported:
"It was a time when it was well for a man to be somewhat
guarded in the remarks he made, what he did with his
hands."[28]

Professional social adjusters took the matter of psychoanalysis seriously. For them it was more than a parlor game, and
more than a method of self-knowledge: it was a social tool.
Even those who sought to maintain their independence of the
Freudian persuasion found many of its concepts useful. Rationalization, repression, sublimation, and transference all had
meaning for people who could not or would not accept
Freudian theory in its entirety.

The outlines of Freudian theory are familiar to most read-
ers, but they bear superficial repetition here for the purpose of
comparison. According to Freud's scheme, the original and
oldest province of the mind contained all of man's instinctual
characteristics. This province he called the id. At birth all the
inherited qualities and no others inhabited the child's undifferentiated id. The specific content of the id was divided
into two categories of unfettered, uncontrolled drives: the
love instinct and the death instinct. "The aim of the first of
these basic instincts is to establish ever greater unities and to
preserve them thus . . . the aim of the second to the contrary is to undo the connections and so to destroy things."[29]
These two instincts sometimes opposed and modified, sometimes combined with one another. The energy of the love
instinct, called the libido, was at first directed entirely toward
the self. As a willing slave to the pleasure principle, the id
remained oblivious to the dangers inherent in its pursuit of
gratification.

In the course of experience with reality, the id developed a
specialized portion, which centered on the faculties of perception and functioned as an intermediary between inner impulses and the demands of reality. This new structure Freud
called the ego. It eschewed the pleasure principle and at-
tended to problems of self-preservation. In its efforts to recon-

cile the id with the outer world, the ego encountered more difficulty with the former than with the latter. "The instincts persist as threats, even if they can be temporarily held in check."[30]

A second agency that functioned to check these persistent impulses arose in turn from the experience of the ego with reality. The additional subdivision of the ego, called the superego, represented the internalized rules of society, especially of the parents, and was commonly referred to as the conscience. As the child grew, its superego gradually incorporated the higher ideals of society as another set of behavioral standards.

In the psychoanalytic interpretation of mental life, morality, the rules of society, restraints upon individual selfishness, far from being inborn, are learned, if ever, only through a terrible struggle. Even the development of the superego and the internalization of parental norms do not nullify the demands of the id. No matter how hard the individual tries, no matter how acceptable and even laudable his overt behavior, there persists within him the struggle between the urges toward life and death and the need to protect himself from the exigencies of the outer world. Crucial patterns of adjustment to conflicting inner and social needs are established very early in the child's life, and the experiences which shape and fix those patterns may be quickly buried in the unconscious.

The early applications of Freudian personality theory to the problem of delinquency yielded results somewhat similar to the untutored assumptions of the juvenile court reformers: the delinquent personality acted out the natural exuberance or amorality of childhood simply because it lacked the restraining influences of proper training and discipline, and the careful attention of loving and conscientious parents. August Aichorn, a pioneering Freudian theorist in deviant behavior, concluded that the delinquent child was lacking in superego. In his important work, *Wayward Youth,* Aichorn wrote:

> It is characteristic of the delinquent that he possess little capacity for repressing instinctual impulses and for directing

energy away from primitive goals. He is thus unable to
achieve what is considered by society a normal ethical code.
The great majority of children in need of retraining come
into conflict with society because of an unsatisfied need for
tenderness and love in their childhood. We therefore find
in them a proportionately increased thirst for pleasure and
for primitive forms of instinctual gratification. They lack
inhibitions and have a strong, distorted craving for affection.[31]

Aichorn recommended the treatment of delinquents as victims
of society whose antagonism to social rules was justified, and
who desired and required a "program of correction based on
love and mutual reconciliation."[32]

This view of the delinquent as victim of an unloving environment suggested that his hostility was a reasonable result of
objective conditions which would presumably yield to a
change in those conditions and to an infusion of affection and
sympathy. Although Freudian in its formulation and embrac-
ing a somewhat more complex vision of human behavior than
that which had animated the juvenile court reformers,
Aichorn's theory was not inconsistent with the optimism
about changing human behavior upon which the court was
built.

At first glance, Freudian theory seemed consistent as well
with the wing of the child-study movement which had seen
the infant as an analogue of the savage. But here we can
begin to see that Freudian psychology reinforced and introduced tendencies more threatening to than supportive of the
premises of the juvenile court movement. Some formulations
of the late-nineteenth-century anthropological view of child
development prefigured the Freudian pessimism about human
raw material. At the 1885 meeting of the National Conference of Charities and Correction, William R. Harris, superintendent of schools for St. Louis, had told an audience:

> It is clear that . . . man can live in society and constitute a
> social whole only so far as individuals are educated out of
> their natural animal condition, and made to respect social
> forms more highly than mere animal impulses. . . . The

family builds up with the child's mind the structures of his moral character, making for him a second nature of moral habit and custom, whose limits and boundaries he regards as of supreme moment.[33]

But the social workers of the twenties who were influenced by psychiatry were less convinced that those of the anthropological wing of the child-study movement that morality belonged as naturally to the adolescent as amorality had to the infant, or that morality could ever become "second nature" to the child, even with long and rigorous training in the demands of the outer world. H. H. Goddard, director of the Ohio Bureau of Juvenile Research, wrote in 1921 that "the evolutionary process of making a useful member of society out of the human child involves a constant modification and control of . . . inherited impulses."[34] The work of a British criminologist published in this country in 1933 observed:

> Poets have extolled the innocence of infancy, the birth-right of each growing boy before the shades of the prison house close over him. The psychologist, the teacher, the harassed parent know too well that moral perfection is no innate gift, but a hard and difficult acquisition.[35]

Of the two wings of the child-study movement, the anthropological faction offered the less flattering view of the child; the Freudian view was less flattering still. Joseph Jastrow, a psychologist at the University of Wisconsin, wrote in 1927: "No child can be permitted to grow up as nature made it and find a desirable place in human society. In this sense the original criminal is the child."[36]

If the first impact of Freudian psychology was to temper optimism about the raw material of childhood and about the ease of shaping that material with social rules, the second was to reinforce the tendency in social workers to turn from an emphasis on family environment to an emphasis on the inner life of clients for clues to behavior problems. Freud's writings warned them that a psychology of the conscious would lead them nowhere and that "the data of conscious perception

which were alone at its disposal have proved themselves in
every respect inadequate to fathom the profusion and com-
plexity of the processes of the mind."[37] The warning was
sympathetically received by a generation of students of behavior who had begun to discover in hypnotism a source of information about the individual that lay beyond the reach of
consciousness. In this uncharted territory of psychic life lay
crucial material for the caseworkers. Roy Lubove writes:

> The revelation [of the unconscious] . . . helps to explain
> the impact of Freudian psychology. Once alerted to the effects
> of the unconscious, it seemed to many social workers that en-
> vironmental manipulation had been based on rationalistic
> assumptions having no relation to the dynamic factors in
> human motivation and behavior.[38]

Freudian ideas also reinforced the trend of social work in
the post-World War I era away from moralism and cen-
soriousness in dealing with behavior problems. Psychoanalytic
theory added greatly to the attractions of moral relativism,
especially by its description of the structure and development
of man's psychic apparatus, which began in the undifferentiated id and culminated only with years of training and experience in the formation of the superego. If morality was not
innate to man, either from infancy or from adolescence, then
the nature of morality, rather than being fixed and universal,
was contingent upon each individual's particular accommodation to a particular social and cultural setting. The point then
was not so much to discover how behavior deviated from
stated moral norms—for the deviation was only a symptom—
but to discover the process of psychic adjustment which had
caused the deviation. Social workers redoubled their efforts to
discuss behavior in functional rather than moral terms.

> Behavior was dynamic, a ceaseless effort to adapt to the pres-
> sures and tensions of the environment. Anti-social behavior
> did not necessarily signify moral perversity, but the sympto-
> matic expression of an unresolved mental conflict or un-
> satisfied inner need. . . .[39]

Although the concept of morality had not altogether outlived its usefulness, the old definition of morality with its specific content now appeared irrelevant to the analysis and treatment of socially unacceptable behavior. And with the attenuation of the significance of the categories of moral and immoral came an attenuation of the significance of the categories normal and abnormal. In an article concerning "The Influence of Psychiatry on Social Work," Dr. F. H. Allen wrote in 1935:

> The mental patient was discovered to be a human being whose sickness was not bizarre and mysterious but had an order and purpose and was related to phenomena observed in so-called normal people.[40]

Freudian theory also brought into question the wisdom of approaching behavior problems with the usual techniques of correctional systems. When the ego functioned to postpone or suppress rather than achieve the gratification of the id, Freud called the process repression. Although Freud frequently pointed out that repression was necessary to social life and that it had produced some of the finest and most creative human works, his audience often took his analysis for an injunction against any disciplinary control of children. Some were led to conclude that repression often resulted in social maladjustment.

Freud did indeed believe that most neuroses among adults derived from the repression of sexual instincts during childhood and that the energy which would have gone into the repressed activity did not dissipate but found some other channel for its release. Thus, although repressed instincts sometimes found productive outlets in artistic or humanitarian endeavor, they also could reappear in unacceptable forms: the repression of aggressive instincts that might have been capable of harmless expression sometimes redirected such energies into antisocial channels. Confusing somewhat Freud's technical meaning of repression as an internal process with the more common meaning of it as a process of external control, some followers of Freud took his concept to discredit discipline. Dr. J. S. Plant, director of the juvenile clinic in Newark, expressed in 1925 the fear of "punishment or its threat as something that but diverts the force of some fundamental drive, which thereupon finds its outlets in an insatiable urge to delinquency."[41]

It was in the context of the Freudian view of the dynamics of behavior that external repression could lead to a dangerous process of internal repression. Far from being random or accidental or even a response to external stimuli, behavior was a purposeful reaction to inner needs. It represented the efforts of the ego to satisfy the demands of the id within society's limits, or if things went awry, beyond those limits. Thus, behavior had a positive function for the individual even if society thought it took a dangerous form. Charles Hoffman, judge of Cincinnati's domestic relations court in 1928, believed that "the *normal* reactions of a child to his particular environment may so affect his person as to make him antisocial in his relations to the home, and the school, and society itself."[42] Unlike the friendly visitors and early probation officers who saw delinquency as the result of bad example or corruption and who therefore had no fear of discouraging it, social workers who followed Freud saw delinquency as the fulfillment of individual needs and desires, a response to an inner drive rather than to environmental temptations and coercions. "Everyone's behavior reflected his emotional needs and represented a more or less successful effort to satisfy them."[43] To thwart behavior, then, was not only to channel energy into unknown activities but also to interrupt the individual's quest for psychic well-being.

The acceptance of Freudian theory had unsettling implications for the juvenile court. The court had been founded on three basic assumptions: the primary innocence of children, social rather than individual responsibility for crime, and the relative ease and clear-cut nature of the reformation process. Freudian psychology denied or modified all three: the child, while perhaps still different from the adult, was no longer sexually pure, no longer instinctively good, no longer free of hostile, aggressive attitudes. While the child as well as the adult still reflected the influence of his emotional environment, he no longer could claim total noncomplicity in the formation of his behavior. In the spirit of a softer determinism, the children themselves achieved the status of *cause* in the constellation of influences that molded their behavior, and they thereby regained a measure of responsibility.

In two senses, then, the delinquent lost that aura of innocence that had quickened so many social consciences. If we remember the importance a somewhat sentimental sympathy for children had as an impetus to reform, we can see how the changing view of the child might affect attitudes toward the juvenile court. Though this change certainly did not signal the abandonment of efforts to rehabilitate delinquents, it did deny the delinquency problem much of its special poignancy and reduce the tolerance of nervous critics for measures that seemed too lenient.

The third premise of the juvenile court system—the ease of reformation—had been constantly challenged by experience. The failure of the court to produce results in rehabilitation had long been apparent. Looking back on the efforts of Chicago women who participated in the early juvenile court movement, Jane Addams recalled that they had disbanded the Juvenile Court Committee which had been so instrumental in securing reform, and in 1906 substituted a Juvenile Protective League to study the social conditions which caused delinquency. She explained the shift in the focus of their efforts by saying, "At least it was apparent that many of these children were psychopathic cases and they and other borderline cases need more skilled care than the most devoted probation could give them."[44] Miss Addams's recollection notwithstanding, it was not until interest in psychology had become much more widespread and the professionalization of social work had gained momentum that the skepticism about ordinary probation work which she attributes to the Chicago women began to be truly telling for the juvenile court. Then the difficulty of reforming child offenders came to be located not in incidental practical deficiencies in the court apparatus but in the nature of the problem itself.

In this respect developments in the psychology of delinquency since Freud have been, if anything, more sobering even than Freudian theory itself. It will be recalled that August Aichorn's early adaption of Freudian theory to the question of delinquency involved only relatively minor alterations in the original juvenile court notion of the genesis of delinquency. As Richard Korn points out, Aichorn and his contemporaries saw the hostility which was expressed in delinquency as derivative:

> Hatred was a response to something else, typically to mistreatment or the withholding of love. By the end of the Second World War, however, hatred had come into its own, as an independent and self-sufficient phenomenon. It was no longer secondary; it did not have to be derived; one did not have to account for it—it was simply there.[45]

Where Aichorn believed that hostility would recede before demonstrations of interest and affection, some later writers have come reluctantly to suspect that such destructive attitudes may be ineradicable.

Fritz Redl and David Wineman undertook in the late forties a field project in the treatment of delinquency in order to test their hypotheses concerning "children who hate" against those of Aichorn's school. After a year and a half of disappointing efforts to reach delinquent children, they published two studies in the early fifties, *Children Who Hate* and *Controls from Within*. They found that some children did indeed seem to misbehave out of confusion and inability to cope with their own instinctive drives. But they found others, far from helpless, who "have an organized system of defenses well developed and meet the adult who tries to change them with a consistent and well-planned barrage of counter-techniques."[46] These children, who seemed not the disoriented victims of a deficiency in life-ordering superego but rather the clever manipulators of adults who tried to reach them, reversed for Redl and Wineman the proposition that children were hostile because they were mistreated. They feared that these children were mistreated because they were hostile, that their hatred was primary rather than derived. Here was a problem for the therapist, and for the juvenile court, which neither had fully contemplated before: a problem child for whom, in Bruno Bettelheim's phrase, "love is not enough," and who stubbornly defends his quest for impulse gratification against feelings of guilt and against the behavior changes which guilt induces. The prognosis for such children—so much more intransigent than those orphaned street urchins and overexuberant children of the lower classes who had goaded the early reformers—could only be more pessimistic.

The discovery of children who hate was not, however, the discovery of a new class of abnormal personalities; rather, it was confirmation of the Freudian suggestion that socially difficult personalities were as fully developed and well defended against change as more socially congenial ones. It was also another step toward considering delinquents normal human beings and, therefore, toward accepting the human category of "criminal" as a permanent feature of social life. The early court reformers had considered the delinquent "normal" in the sense that he was capable of adopting and abiding by middle-class norms. Delinquency, not the delinquent, was abnormal. They tended, however, to regard the delinquent child as somehow incomplete, either psychologically or culturally, or both. The cultural incompletion made him a threat to society, but the psychological incompletion made it possible to reform him by exposure to good example and exhortation. The very optimism of the juvenile court movement rested on the assumption that given a fair choice between middle-class values and any others, the normal human being—one who was not biologically doomed—would choose the middle-class way.

Over the course of the twentieth century, however, the dominant trend of psychology has been to regard behavior, antisocial or otherwise, as only the visible aspect of deep and complex emotional patterns which become available to the understanding only through expert investigation and amenable to modification only with long-term effort. The kind of therapy implied by this sort of analysis of human behavior is very different from what the juvenile court reformers intended to build into their system and, indeed, from what public resources are ever likely to provide for the delinquent population. To claim for courtroom procedure—however informal and sympathetic—or standard probation work the term "therapeutic" once psychiatry had come of age was to sound naïve indeed.

Alongside this trend in the development of psychology has run a development in thinking about the sociology of deviance which has been equally significant in discrediting the fundamental notions of the juvenile court.

6

SOCIOLOGY

As skepticism about the innate goodness or even the malleability of juvenile offenders has developed among theorists of the delinquent personality, a parallel skepticism has developed among those who concentrate on the social milieu and cultural genesis of delinquency. From the sociology of deviance there has emerged a picture of modern industrial society in which crime and delinquency seem to have a natural and perhaps a permanent place.

There was in the literature of the early juvenile court movement a rudimentary form of what has become a theory (or several theories) of a delinquency subculture. But very rudimentary it was. Delinquency in the late nineteenth and early twentieth centuries may have appeared vicious in practice, but depravity, in theory, was not behind it. The delinquent was at worst an amoral embryo of a moral adult who had been temporarily distracted from his normal development by the forces of disorder or deprivation around him. One of those forces, one of the distractions, might be "bad companions." Reformers presumably thought the street children who had no homes and, therefore, no adult supervision fell too much under the influence of other footloose children. The juvenile reformatories from which reformers wished to save the children through probation were breeding grounds for crime presumably in part because children were capable of

acculturating each other to deviant social patterns. The reformers who participated in the early juvenile court movement thus did contemplate the possibility that peer-group
influence as well as the unsavory example of adults might encourage misbehavior. It seems, however, that the weakness of
adult supervision rather than the persuasiveness of a peer culture was for them the key to the delinquency puzzle. The
weakness of adult supervision might appear to have something
to do with lower-class culture, but in the minds of the early
reformers, it seems to have had more to do with the direct
effects of poverty in a sort of cultural vacuum. Insofar as the
sources of crime were "social," the relevant social unit was the
family, which a probation officer might enter and set right
without serious competition from another set of values.

While the early reformers sought the cause of delinquency
in impersonal social forces, placing responsibility for crime on
the society rather than the individual, they nevertheless
planned to work with individuals, to practice reformation on
one child at a time. Feeling sympathetic and protective as well
as somewhat threatened by these children whose lives had
been twisted by bad environment, the reformers had the
choice either to follow their logic into the fray between good
and evil and to remake the society without the forces which
produced crime, or to stand on the sidelines and administer
first aid to the children who were the battle's victims. The
early court advocates chose the rescue operation rather than
the root-and-branch approach for reasons we may surmise:
because it seemed easier; because the role of the child saver
had much appeal; and because, if they recognized the man-
date for social change implied in their analysis, they did not
really want to carry it out. If they glimpsed in the physical
and economic conditions of the slums anything resembling a
cultural superstructure, it had no depth and certainly nothing
that might be positive or functional even for its participants.

The seeds of a subculture theory of delinquency can be
found in the works of Clifford Shaw and Henry MacKay,
foremost among them the book *Delinquency Areas,* published

in 1929, and *Social Factors in Delinquency*, published as part of the Report of the Causes of Crime of the National Commission on Law Observance in 1931. Explorers of the proposition that crime and delinquency had geographic centers, Shaw and MacKay are often cited as pathfinders in social transmission theories of deviance. In the 1930's, Healy and Bronner and others who interested themselves in street gangs began to notice a contrast between the purposefulness of adult crime and the malicious gratuitousness of delinquency.[1] They were thus moving toward a picture of delinquency as a pattern of behavior with a special social organization and with distinct values and norms. But it has been particularly since the Second World War that subculture theories of delinquency have flourished. These theories have come a long way from allusions to the influence of bad companions.

Much of the literature on delinquency of the mid-century shared the social orientation of the early reformers, but regarded the social patterns of delinquency as purposeful, tenacious, and normal in their social context, based on long and complex learning processes and involving allegiances as strong as anyone ever felt for the values of the middle class. Unlike the early orientation, which considered delinquency abnormal because it was immoral by middle-class standards, and unlike the orientation of the twenties, which considered delinquency a matter of maladjustment, the sociology of deviance tends to depict delinquent behavior as a natural adjustment to the life conditions which surround many children as they grow up. And more important, it does not dismiss those life conditions as merely temporary aberrations, the accidents of recent urbanization or immigration. Nor does it imagine that such conditions can long persist without generating their own values and norms. Post-Second World War subculture theories do what the early reformers could never have contemplated: they emphasize the existence of another set of values and another order of allegiances which, if anything, have the advantage in the battle for the future of young offenders. Not "bad" companions, but companions in a sub-

culture with its own roles and rewards lie behind delinquency. As Albert Cohen, a leading exponent of subculture
theory, wrote in 1955:

> A large and growing number of students of juvenile de-
> linquency . . . believes that the only important difference
> between the delinquent and the non-delinquent is the degree
> of exposure to this delinquent culture pattern. They hold
> that the delinquent is not distinguished by any special stig-
> mata, physical or psychological. Some delinquents are bright,
> some are slow; some are seriously frustrated, some are not;
> some have grave mental conflicts and some do not. And the
> same is true of non-delinquents. . . . The process of be-
> coming a delinquent is the same as the process of becoming,
> let us say, a Boy Scout. The difference lies only in the culture
> pattern with which the child associates.[2]

Just as some theorists of the delinquent personality discovered that their subjects were not simply confused and helpless, lacking in superego, but had a strong and complex
psychic structure fully comparable to the nondelinquent's, so
theorists of the cultural genesis of delinquency discovered that
it was not a lack of moral rules or social organization but a
different set of moral rules and social organization that lay
behind the deviance. Cohen writes: "In the 'delinquency area'
as elsewhere, there is an awareness of community, an involvement of the individual in the lives and doings of the neigh-
borhood, a concern about his reputation among his neighbors.
. . . The qualities and defects of organization are not to be
confused with the absence of organization."[3]

Just as the theorists of the delinquent personality by mid-
century tended to consider their subjects for the most part not
just potentially but actually normal people, the subculture
analysts felt certain that a delinquency subculture existed and
that "it [was] a normal, integral, and deeply rooted feature of
the social life of the modern American city."[4] These conces-
sions made the problem of delinquency, in the individual as
well as in the social context, manifestly more resistant to solution than it had appeared at the time the juvenile court was

created. If the delinquent is not simply off the one-and-only track, but is on an alternative track, one which runs at cross-purposes to the dominant social order, it will be much more difficult to redirect him.

Some contemporary social transmission theories of delinquency, echoing the much less sophisticated turn-of-the-century identification of crime with poverty, suggest that delinquency is merely the adolescent manifestation of lower-class culture. In the metaphor of Albert Cohen, the attitudes of the lower class, especially its "short-run hedonism," are "the fabric . . . of which delinquency is the most brilliant and spectacular thread."[5] Walter B. Miller suggests that in a lower-class culture which rewards toughness and smartness, and celebrates luck, excitement, and freedom from external restraint, children are virtually encouraged to engage in illegal acts. Delinquency is purposeful, positive, and culturally normal in this setting. According to Miller:

> No culture pattern as well established as the practice of illegal acts by members of lower-class corner groups could persist if buttressed primarily by negative, hostile, or rejective motives; its principal motivation support, as in the case of any persisting cultural tradition, derives from a positive effort to achieve what is valued within that tradition, and conform to its explicit norms.[6]

There is a difference of opinion among subculture theorists as to the relationship between lower-class culture and its adolescent variant on the one hand and middle-class culture on the other. Though they may accept the assertion that the practices of delinquent subcultures are motivated by positive as well as negative impulses, some writers, Cohen among them, describe the content of the delinquency subculture as a rejection of the dominant culture and inversion of its values. "The hallmark of the delinquent subculture is the explicit and wholesale repudiation of middle-class standards and the adoption of their very antitheses."[7] This subculture, then, "is not only a set of rules, a design for living which is different from or indifferent to or even in conflict with the norms of the 'respectable' adult society. It would appear at least plausible that it is defined by its 'negative polarity' to those norms. . . . The delinquent's conduct is right, by the standards of his subculture, precisely *because* it is wrong by the norms of the larger culture."[8] The very source of delinquency would thus be the desire to act out the total rejection of middle-class taboos.

> It is precisely here . . . in the refusal to temporize, that the appeal of the delinquent subculture lies. . . . As long as the working-class . . . boy clings to a version, however attenuated and adulterated, of the middle-class culture, he must recognize his inferiority. . . . The delinquent subculture, on the other hand, permits no ambiguity of the status of the delinquent relative to that of anybody else. In terms of the norms of the delinquent subculture, defined by its polarity to the respectable status system, the delinquent's very non-conformity to middle-class standards sets him above the most exemplary college boy.[9]

This leads us to another parallel between current psychogenic and subcultural theories—besides the observation in both of the normality and tenacity of delinquent patterns—which contributes to the growing pessimism concerning delinquency and its elimination. The underived hostility, observed by Redl and Wineman, which refuses to respond to conditions of love and interest and seems to blanket and smother relations with the delinquent personality, appears analogously in the content of the delinquent subculture as the ornery, purposeless form which so much delinquent activity takes on. In the literature of delinquency subcultures that gratuitous individual hostility is paralleled by the inexplicable and purposeless vandalism which is to occupy the time of so many juvenile offenders. Cohen writes:

> What we see when we look at the delinquent subculture (and we must not even assume that this describes all juvenile delinquency) is that it is *non-utilitarian, malicious,* and

negativistic. . . . In homelier language, stealing "for the hell of it" and apart from considerations of gain and profit is a valued activity to which attaches glory, prowess, and profound satisfaction. There is no accounting in rational and utilitarian terms for the effort expended and the danger run in stealing things which are often discarded, destroyed, or casually given away.[10]

As Cohen observes, earlier writers had occasionally noticed this aspect of the culture of delinquent gangs. But the maturation of the insight indicates a significant shift from the relatively sympathetic assumption that poor children stole in order to gain possession of things—some of them necessary, some of them merely desired—which other children enjoyed but which they were denied by virtue of their poverty.

Cohen's version of the theory of a delinquency subculture emphasizes the distance between the values of the middle and lower classes and thereby contrasts with the optimistic assumptions by early reformers of the natural appeal of their own mores. It has been criticized for several reasons, among them its failure to deal with the fact that delinquents exhibit feelings of shame and guilt which belie a total rejection of middle-class standards.[11] An approach which avoids this problem while still contending that status frustration is the source of delinquency suggests that delinquency is merely an overemphasis on middle-class, respectable goals. When children who share the goals of the dominant culture discover that they cannot achieve those goals by approved means, rather than abandon the goals, they adopt unconventional means of attaining them. Sociologist Robert K. Merton contended as early as 1938 that "certain aspects of the social structure may generate . . . anti-social behavior precisely because of differential emphasis on goals and regulations. In the extreme case, the latter may be so vitiated by the goal-emphasis that the range of behavior is limited only by considerations of technical expediency."[12] In situations where economic and educational deprivation combine with a cultural devotion to the accumulation of wealth as a symbol of success, antisocial conduct is a "normal" response. "In societies such as our own, then, the pressure of prestige-bearing success tends to eliminate the effective social constraint over means employed to this end."[13] For children who started out in pursuit of the dominant goals but found their road blocked, crime offered another standard against which to measure themselves, an alternate route to self-esteem. By this reckoning, as long as the culture continued to measure success by the accumulation of scarce resources—resources which only some individuals would be able to secure legitimately—we could expect to find people trying to secure them illegitimately.

Whether the delinquency subculture is just an adolescent variant of a lower-class culture, or is an inversion of middle-class culture, or is the result of an overemphasis on the goals of middle-class culture at the expense of its accepted means, this literature tells us that delinquency proceeds from a tradition of its own with functions and satisfactions of its own. It is not to be regarded as existing in a cultural vacuum which a probation officer can fill. The theorists of a delinquency subculture, like the theorists of a delinquent personality, do not contend that the patterns they describe exhaust or embrace all instances of antisocial behavior among juveniles: they leave room for other analyses and other categories of causation. But they do insist that the patterns they describe are real, that there *are* subcultures which define or pursue their "goods" by the "bads" of the dominant society, and that there *are* personalities which are fundamentally hostile and deliberately unreachable.

To a problem of such psychological and sociological dimensions, the juvenile court apparatus must seem largely irrelevant. It has, however, also seemed worse than irrelevant in the context of other work coming out of the sociological tradition. Some critics of the subculture theory have suggested that there is a fatal internal contradiction in such institutions as the juvenile court which not only make them ineffective but make them counterproductive in the effort to control and reduce deviance. The position is well illustrated by the work of Gresham Sykes and David Matza.

Focusing on one moment in the evolution of delinquents

and criminals, Matza and Sykes, in an article published in 1957, argued that the key to deviance lies in the process by which delinquent behavior becomes a permissible means to conventional goals.[14] They called the process "neutralization," and at its center they found the issue of responsibility. They said that if a child could by some means sever the link of responsibility between his actions and legal norms, he was able to engage in criminal activity without losing his self-esteem and without abandoning the value system which condemned his behavior. The techniques by which he divested himself of responsibility were themselves learned from the dominant culture. Before he committed a forbidden act, rather than as an after-the-fact rationalization, the delinquent decided that his act would not really do any harm, that his intended victim deserved it anyway, that higher loyalties demanded violation of the rules, that for some reason under those circumstances the forbidden behavior was all right. So opened the way to crime.

Thus far, the explanation of neutralization is universal, not dependent upon particular life conditions. In a book on neutralization theory published in 1964, Matza provided a connection between this universal process and the special circumstances of young people who harbor resentments against material or cultural deprivation.

> The delinquent is prepared to convert irresponsibility into freedom from moral constraint because his subculture is pervaded by another more profound condition of neutralization. This additional condition—a sense of injustice—. . . provides a simmering resentment . . . within which the variety of extenuating circumstances may abrogate the moral bond to law.[15]

The role of the sense of injustice in causing delinquency has led the proponents of this theory to a condemnation of the juvenile court. While other theories of delinquency may have suggested the irrelevance of the court to solving the problem, proponents of the neutralization theory saw the juvenile court itself as an irritant of the problem and a further cause of recidivism. Writing in 1967 for the President's Commission on Law Enforcement and the Administration of Justice, Edwin Lemert found: "The conclusion that the court processing . . . in some way helps to fix and perpetuate delinquency in many cases is hard to escape."[16]

One of the ways in which the court allegedly helped to perpetuate delinquency was its effect upon the child's self-definition: by virtue of the court experience, the child came to think of himself as delinquent, and thenceforth found it easier to accept in himself the behavior associated with delinquency. Any judicial conviction, however, in juvenile court or elsewhere, would threaten this effect on self-definition, and the problem is unavoidable if the community's need for protection is to be considered at all.

More crucial to the juvenile court was the suggestion made by proponents of the neutralization theory that the court itself underlined and fostered the very feelings which allowed delinquents to exempt themselves from legal rules in the first place. The juvenile court's most obvious mistake in this regard lay in the positivist criminology it preached: that the child himself is not responsible for his delinquent act and that society must be held accountable. The court made its second mistake by not practicing what it preached: while its rhetoric referred to social responsibility, it convicted and incarcerated the individual delinquent and did nothing to punish the delinquent society, thus fostering the sense of injustice. In a situation where "the avoidance of hypocrisy is paramount," the court was obviously guilty of hypocrisy.

> We may not without consequence assign fault to the larger collectivity and penal sanction to the individual member. The consequence of such discrepancies between theory and practice are heightened in institutions that require the consent of subordinates. The juvenile court is such an institution. The juvenile court requires a greater grant of legitimacy from its clientele than previous courts because its aspirations are loftier. . . . The capacity to accept treatment depends on the trust accorded the court and its agents. Hypocrisy—saying one thing and doing another—is fundamentally corrosive of

trust. . . . By its insistence on a philosophy of child welfare and its addiction to word magic, the juvenile court systematically interferes with its alleged program.[17]

The court's final error lay in the preaching and practice of individualized justice. While social workers may have had elaborate rationales for this approach, it appeared to the delinquent to be an unfair and capricious system which sent him to the reformatory for stealing while his friend went free on probation for the same offense. Having first encouraged the child offender to exempt himself of responsibility, and having then squandered its moral capital by its hypocrisy, the court completed the necessary conditions for neutralization by administering a system of individualized dispositions which reinforced the delinquent's sense of injustice. All this "support[s] the process by which the moral bond of law is neutralized" and "facilitates the drift into delinquency."[18]

If this analysis is correct, the juvenile court reformers not only failed in the effort to reduce delinquency but set the effort back. For Matza, the analysis served to discredit positivist criminology and individualized justice. A similar analysis has led others to criticize particularly as counterproductive the informal procedure and pretense to paternalism which is associated with the *parens patriae* doctrine. Wheeler and Cottrell have argued that the contrast between the rhetoric and the reality, where it exists, of the informal approach in court and the sternness of the sanctions which may follow it creates an atmosphere of distrust which interferes with rehabilitative efforts. They write that "unless appropriate due process of law is followed, even the juvenile who has violated the law may not feel that he is being fairly treated and may therefore resist the rehabilitative efforts of court personnel."[19] The Report of the President's Commission on Law Enforcement and the Administration of Justice reached a similar conclusion in 1967:

There is increasing evidence that the informal procedures, contrary to the original expectations, may themselves constitute a further obstacle to effective treatment of the delinquent to the extent that they engender in the child a sense of injustice provoked by seemingly all-powerful and challengeless exercise of authority by judges and probation officers.[20]

The extreme criticism that views positivist criminology, individualized justice, and informal procedure as approaches which exacerbate the problem of delinquency has not pushed from the field psychogenic and subcultural interpretations of delinquency. These interpretations remain influential and imply only the more moderate criticism that the juvenile court and its probation arm are inadequate rather than inimical to the rehabilitative ideal. They are, however, a more serious challenge to the juvenile court than were the first criticisms, which concentrated on the distance between the ideal juvenile court and the real. While the theoretical criticism of the juvenile court has become increasingly profound, the practical criticisms have continued unabated. Together they have had the effect of creating yet another crisis of confidence in our institutions for dealing with juvenile crime.

CONCLUSION:
LOSING THE FAITH

In the late nineteenth and early twentieth centuries, the voices of social control and liberal reform spoke as one in favor of a new court for children and a new definition of delinquency. The movement for change in the juvenile justice system in the progressive period cast the effort to prevent crime and rehabilitate delinquents in the form of a court, but a court which was to resemble as little as possible those familiar in the criminal law. This new system of juvenile justice would eschew fixed and specific definitions of offenses for general findings of delinquency. It would likewise eschew fixed prescriptions for the treatment of delinquency. It would be organized instead as a flexible, adaptable mechanism for the continuous, expert supervision of delinquent and pre-delinquent children, broadly defined, until their majority. By means of a fusion of efficiency and humanitarianism it would prevent, cure, and reduce crime.

By the late 1960's the spokesmen for crime control and humanitarian reform no longer spoke with one voice. They did, however, agree from their respective positions that the juvenile justice system had strayed too far from the criminal justice model. The return to that model, if still incomplete, nevertheless suggests a profound loss of faith both in the juvenile court idea and in the approach to social problems which it exemplified by its confidence in the fluid, scientific exercise of discretion.

The first signs of disappointment with the juvenile court came early, if in moderate form. Roughly at the end of the first decade of experience with the juvenile court in action, a number of people felt called upon to look back on its record to date and to conclude that it was "not, alas, a cure-all."[1] Judge Lindsey himself confessed in 1910 his disappointment that, though much had been achieved through the informal procedures of the juvenile court and probation, they had proven mere "palliatives" for the problem of delinquency.[2] In her introduction to a study of the first ten years of the Chicago juvenile court, Julia Lathrop, who had participated so enthusiastically in the founding of the court, concluded that "while the study gives reason for going forward in the direction already taken it shows no cure-all."[3]

Well into the 1920's, most of the court's critics seemed inclined to allow that the court was still in its formative stages, still had potential, still had a contribution to make. In 1921, addressing the Children's Bureau Conference on Juvenile Court Standards, Lathrop repeated her disappointing assessment and her appeal to continue in the same direction:

> We have laws providing juvenile courts in 46 states and providing juvenile probation in all the states save one; but our performance lags behind our laws. The juvenile court is 22 years old; we can never revert from its idea. Is it not possible to awaken fresh interest in a nation-wide realization of its ideal of justice?[4]

In the face of systematic inquiries into the actual deficiencies of the juvenile court, the characteristic response may have been, with Lathrop, to redouble efforts to realize the juvenile court ideal. As late as 1931, the National Commission on Law Observance and Enforcement (the Wickersham Commission) found that the juvenile court had not succeeded in providing the services it had promised, but still supported its fundamental conception.

At the same time, however, impatience was growing with these exhortations to try yet again the same means to the same ends. In 1924, Miriam Van Waters spoke to the National Conference of Social Work:

> I cannot refrain from repeating the profound saying of Santayana in describing fanatics. Are we not ourselves, in this delinquency business, something of fanatics? "Fanatics are those who redouble their efforts—when they have forgotten their aim."[5]

The aim remained, as Van Waters knew, to rehabilitate the juvenile offender. But in the late 1920's and 1930's it began to seem possible that the juvenile court was fatally flawed as a means to the end of rehabilitation.

The genius of the juvenile court had been its combination of judicial and therapeutic functions, and the blurring of distinctions between them. In the twenties and thirties judges like Herbert M. Baker of Colorado and E. F. Waite of Minnesota, clinic directors like Dr. William Healy and Dr. Frederick Allen, social scientists like Thomas D. Eliot and social workers like Henrietta Additon and Emma Lundberg declared that there existed a disabling incongruity between the judicial and therapeutic functions. Dr. Allen complained of the juvenile court's confusion of roles before the National Probation Association in 1929:

> There is an essential incongruity between the more common sense, scientific approach which regards behavior as emerging from a variety of factors and the approach which is judgmental and seeks to change behavior through external pressure. . . . It seems necessary to me to get away from the incongruity that exists in our present day efforts to combine in a juvenile court the power "to punish" and the capacity "to treat."[6]

Responding to Dr. Allen's paper in discussion, a juvenile court probation officer spoke of the practical effects of the dilemma:

The case worker connected with the court has constantly to overcome false ideas as to the function and purpose of the court. Many parents and children feel that the probation officer is making an investigation in order to fix blame for misdeeds and administer punishment. They feel it is a disgrace to have a probation officer calling at their home and will do anything they can to cover up any fact which they consider might be used against the child.[7]

Simply put, the lesson of the psychotherapeutic approach to delinquency seemed to be that the juvenile court was fundamentally unsuited to the task of rehabilitation because it was inescapably a court of law.

The key premise in the argument that the juvenile court was unsuited to its task held that human behavior was exceedingly complex and that to change it required a sustained and intimate relationship between the subject and a trained therapist. The court apparatus itself was utterly helpless in such a long, complex, and personal process. Even where courts had at their disposal the services of trained therapists, their techniques had proven curiously ineffectual in dealing with the problem of delinquency when they were practiced under the aegis of the court.

> The addition of the psychiatrist and improvement in the probation services have not resulted in the increased percentage of "cures" by the courts that was expected. As a result, the findings of all the reports of recent studies of the results obtained by the juvenile courts have been very discouraging to those who hoped that the juvenile court would, if not prevent, at least greatly reduce delinquency.[8]

For those who believed, as so many social workers were coming to believe, that behavior could be changed most effectively, and perhaps only, by means of psychiatric procedures, the question arose why such procedures had not worked in the limited trials they had received in the context of the juvenile court.

The answer toward which they began to lean was disturbing: perhaps the court setting was inherently unsuited to psychiatric treatment; perhaps what the delinquent child needed, a court could not give. The only constructive relationship between patient and therapist rested of necessity on trust; without such trust the depth of self-examination and revelation which was necessary to behavior change could not occur. And the crushing "discovery" of the period (though perhaps the insight of relatively few observers) was that because of his affiliation with an institution of punishment, an agent of the court, even if he was a trained therapist, might in most cases be incapable of securing the faith of his patient, who was, after all, also a defendant.

If, in the opinion of some professional therapists, the judicial context confused and undermined the therapeutic effort, therapeutic considerations had a similar effect on the proper functioning of a court. Judge Baker wrote as early as 1920 about the "failure" of the juvenile court:

> The reasons for this failure are many. Among them are poorly conceived laws, inadequate equipment both personal and material, and incompetent judges; but by far the most salient reason is that courts are not fundamentally adapted to this work. . . . The true function of a court is to determine judicially the facts at issue before it. . . . Investigations into the lives, environments, or heredity of delinquents, the infliction of punishment and the supervision of probation . . . are repugnant to every tenet of the science of law.[9]

The cost of grafting therapeutic functions onto a court of law was to hamper it in the performance of the only service it had to render.

For those whose professional orientation was therapeutic, the solution to this confusion of contradictory roles took the form of removing the therapeutic and preventive functions from the juvenile court. The most popular idea—with which legal critics could agree—suggested untangling the warring functions by transferring prevention and rehabilitation to the schools. In the education system teachers and administrators

could observe the signs of incipient delinquency early enough
to control it. If children slipped through the schools' preventive net and ended in juvenile court, they could return to the
schools for reeducation and rehabilitation. In 1922, a committee on juvenile courts of the National Probation Association
proposed that a resolution be directed to professional educa-
tors and the United States Bureau of Education approving in
principle of the

> gradual assumption by the education system of . . . re-
> sponsibility for the study and treatment of malbehavior prob-
> lems as primarily educational or reeducational problems; and
> . . . that this be made possible by means of adequate special
> equipment and personnel attached to the educational system,
> so as to relieve the probation officers and courts of much extra
> burden for which they are not adequately prepared and
> should not be expected to assume responsibility.[10]

Although this idea had considerable support within the association and without, the resolution did not pass and the proposal embodied in it came to naught. Nevertheless, the repeated suggestion of it revealed a serious loss of faith in the
court's capacity to deal with the problem for which it had
been created. Such reliance upon an institution neither designed nor equipped for rehabilitation indicated the desperation with which at least some critics cast about in the 1920's
and thirties for alternatives to the juvenile court system.

For Judge Baker the educational alternative was not radical
enough. In 1921, he proposed to remove both the judicial and
the therapeutic functions from the juvenile court.

> The purely judicial function of determining whether or not
> a child is delinquent could just as well be discharged by the
> courts formerly in existence. . . . If the child should be
> found delinquent, he should be remanded to the proper au-
> thorities for treatment. . . . As it is, so far as I know not a
> single court is doing this work well; and in my opinion, no
> court constituted as juvenile courts are now constituted, can
> do it well.[11]

While what troubled Judge Baker primarily was the mutually debilitating effects which adjudicative and therapeutic functions had upon each other, he was also concerned with the discretion which the role of "therapist" gave the person who had also to act as judge. He worried that "not even under 'chancery powers' have courts heretofore been endowed with administrative authority of this kind."[12] Shortly thereafter, Judge Edward F. Waite raised the same question in an article entitled "How Far Can Court Procedure Be Socialized without Impairing Individual Rights?"[13] and another critic observed that "there is a check on the authority which the judge wields in adult courts, but there is very little, if any, control now being exercised over juvenile court judges. . . ."[14] Nevertheless, the suggestion that the adjudicative function of the juvenile court be returned to the criminal courts had no more practical impact than did the suggestion that the therapeutic functions be transferred to the schools. Even more moderate suggestions for granting some procedural protections to children in juvenile court went unheeded in the twenties and thirties. The representation of the juvenile court as a danger to liberty led up a blind alley which was not to open until the 1960's.

The idea that the juvenile court might be a danger of another sort did, however, gain some currency in the 1930's and did motivate some minor informal and legislative changes during the next thirty years. This was the danger that the juvenile court might not only fail to eradicate patterns of delinquency but, by labeling and stigmatizing children, might actually fix such patterns in the children which it sought to cure. In 1930 a professor of sociology explained how it might happen:

> A boy cannot be a delinquent without thinking of himself as a delinquent. Every contact that he makes impresses him with this fact. . . . A child who can be spared a court experience may escape recriminations and threats of incarceration in an industrial school or some other institution. Appearance in court places a stigma on the child and gives him a pernicious definition of himself.[15]

Some judges and social workers also noticed the negative effects of a finding of delinquency both on the child's reputation and on his opinion of himself. Their notice acknowledged the failure of the juvenile court movement to eliminate from juvenile proceedings the stigma which attached to criminal convictions, and foreshadowed the development of labeling theory. The best practical suggestion to deal with this problem was to keep children out of court as much as possible, and to make rehabilitative services available to them without benefit of formal court action. In part as a response to this suggestion, the juvenile court case load handled out of court, largely by probation officers, climbed to and leveled at about 50 percent as a national average, and much higher in some jurisdictions.

Also in response to problems of labeling and stigma, the National Council on Crime and Delinquency began in 1943, with the fourth edition of its Standard Juvenile Court Act, to omit all reference to the term "delinquent." Commenting upon the continued omission of the term in 1959 in the sixth edition of the Standard Act, the council wrote that the form "accords with the philosophy that, in dealing with the child as an individual, classifying or labelling him is always unnecessary, sometimes impracticable, and often harmful."[16] In 1959, about one third of the states had adopted the council's non-labeling approach.

Another group of states approached the labeling problem by creating a new label for children who indulged in noncriminal behavior that came under the jurisdiction of the court. New York, New Jersey, and Illinois, for example, carved out of the delinquency jurisdiction those "offenses" which would not be criminal if committed by an adult and named the children who committed them "Minors (or Children or Persons) in Need of Supervision." New York's Family Court Act in 1962 reserved the label "juvenile delinquent" for children between seven and sixteen who committed any act which if done by an adult would constitute a crime. It created the new label "Person in Need of Supervision" for habitual truants, and for children whose behavior was incorrigible, ungovernable, habitually disobedient, or who were beyond the lawful control of their parents.[17]

These legislative changes which, like the preference for unofficial handling of cases, suggested the deleterious consequences of court appearances and delinquency adjudications nevertheless fell short of a comprehensive indictment capable of eliciting change in the juvenile court process itself. If they did anything at all to solve the problem of stigma, they did nothing to reduce the level of interventionism which the juvenile court movement had encouraged. While they surely suggest waning confidence in the juvenile court as a rehabilitative agency in its own right, they did not indicate doubt that some agency could assemble the scientific knowledge and skill to change behavior. They did nothing to narrow the definition of juvenile court jurisdiction or to suggest that it should be narrowed. They erected no barriers to court intervention in the lives of children once they appeared in juvenile court. They did not suggest that at some point the failure of the juvenile court to live up to the reformers' ideal had to be accepted as fact and that the acceptance had to become the basis for change in the court itself. The observations of pernicious effects of court appearances fed into what had become, by the time of the Great Depression, a formidable battery of criticism, but for the next twenty or thirty years, the argument against the juvenile court did not gel. Before that could happen, more experience, more theorizing, and a shift in values surrounding the criminal law process would be necessary.

Neither the 1930's—which were so largely devoted to struggling against unemployment and economic collapse—nor the 1940's—which were so largely devoted to the war effort—left much energy for juvenile justice reform. Insofar as youth received special attention during the Depression, they received it as a subgroup for relief and reemployment efforts. With recovery in the early war years, attention was again distracted from reform efforts in juvenile justice, except for the rather frail attempts described above to mitigate the effects of labeling. But during the forties and fifties some of the ingredients which would be necessary to solidify serious disaffection from the juvenile court ideal began to appear.

One of the ingredients came from the impression of a continually increasing rate of juvenile crime. During the war, according to the statistics gathered by the Children's Bureau, delinquency rates as measured both by FBI arrest records and by juvenile court case loads made a large jump. After dropping considerably in the period immediately following the war, the rate again began to climb, and continued to do so in virtually every year after 1949. Between 1957 and 1965, the Children's Bureau records indicated that the increase in delinquency cases was 58 percent, almost double the increase in the child population.[18]

As the incidence of delinquency seemed continually on the rise, the explanations of delinquency put the problem ever further out of the reach of a court. During the 1950's, the subcultural school of delinquency theory pointed to causes lying in social conditions so broad and deep that they seemed to mock efforts to cure delinquents by informal court procedure and probation.

In the meantime, the news concerning the gap between ideal and real in juvenile court offered no more encouragement than such news ever had. There is no reason here to detail the recent observations, since they so closely resemble those made as early as the 1920's. It will do perhaps to say that various national and local commissions and other chroniclers of the juvenile court continued in the 1960's to report on the inadequacy of the preparation of juvenile court judges, on the small number (roughly 10 percent of 2,987) of juvenile court judges who devoted full time to juvenile matters, on the persistent incarceration of children in adult institutions, on the lack of detention, probation, and diagnostic facilities, and on the high rate of recidivism among juvenile offenders.[19]

Perhaps the most influential study of the juvenile courts was published in 1967 by the President's Commission on Law Enforcement and the Administration of Justice in its report, *The Challenge of Crime in a Free Society*. The commission concluded: "The juvenile court has not succeeded significantly in rehabilitating delinquent youth, in reducing or even stemming the tide of delinquency, or in bringing justice and compassion to the child offender."[20] The commission did not stop, however, as so many other critics had, with the observation of the gap between the real and the ideal. It blamed the existence of that gap in part on community unwillingness to provide necessary resources, but it also took seriously sociological research which suggested that even a massive infusion of resources would not solve the problem.

> What research is making increasingly clear is that delinquency is not so much an act of individual deviancy as a pattern of behavior which is induced by a multitude of pervasive societal influences well beyond the reach of actions by any judge, probation officer, correctional counsellor or psychiatrist.[21]

And, most importantly, the commission concluded that change was necessary, change that would be "based on the recognition that in the past our reach has exceeded our grasp."[22]

For at least three decades before the commission's report was published, the cup of the juvenile court had seemed half full. The report made clear that by the mid-1960's the cup appeared half empty. The ingredient which brought about this change in perception was a rise of due process values—an increased concern with individual liberty and a skepticism about the benevolence of state intervention even in the "best interests of the child." The impact of due process thinking can be seen in some of the commission's recommendations. Beyond the already commonplace suggestion that as many children as possible be handled without official court action, the commission recommended narrowing the definition of delinquency to exclude noncriminal conduct. It concluded that even efforts to "help" children must be based on facts proving delinquency and that the best way to ascertain facts was the judicial trial constrained by the sorts of safeguards for the defendant which apply in criminal trials. The impact of due process thinking can be seen more dramatically

in a series of decisions in which the Supreme Court provided
a way to measure the significance of the juvenile court's persistent failure to deliver on its promise to juvenile offenders
and to the community.

When, in 1966, the Supreme Court issued its first decision
concerning a juvenile court, it had available to it a body
of opinion—judicial, legislative, and scholarly—in favor of
bringing juvenile court procedure under some constitutional
control. But in that first case, *Kent v. U.S.*, the Court confined itself to statutory rather than constitutional require-
ments in assessing the validity of a procedure to waive
juvenile court jurisdiction in favor of a criminal court in the
District of Columbia. Between 1967 and 1974, however, the
Court decided four major cases concerning constitutional
rights in juvenile court: *In re Gault, In re Winship,
McKeiver et al. v. Pennsylvania,* and *Breed v. Jones.* In only
one of them (*McKeiver*) did the Court fail to amplify and
expand the application of due process concepts to the juvenile
court. In these decisions the Court brought together many of
the observations which had been made by practical, theoretical, and procedural critics. It has been said, with some merit,
that even taken together the decisions do not provide a
coherent jurisprudence for the juvenile justice system.[23] But
they do indicate the significant respects in which thinking
about that system and about the problem which it was designed to solve has departed from notions upon which the
juvenile court was created.

The most important difference between the Supreme
Court's approach to the juvenile court and the approach taken
by courts of review in the early twentieth century lay in the
Court's unwillingness to allow mere invocation of *parens
patriae* doctrine to dispose of procedural challenges. While the
Court in *Kent* felt it unnecessary and therefore unwise to
reach constitutional questions, it did warn that "the admoni-
tion to function in a 'parental' relationship is not an invitation
to procedural arbitrariness."[24] In *Gault,* the Court faced more
directly the capacity of *parens patriae* doctrine to justify the
denial of constitutional rights in juvenile court.

Gault was the first and broadest of the cases concerning the adjudicative stage of juvenile court proceedings. The case came to the Supreme Court on appeal from the supreme court of Arizona. There, the parents of Gerald Gault, a minor, had again failed to win a writ of *habeas corpus* for their son's release from the Arizona Industrial School to which he had been committed in 1964 for making lewd phone calls. Although the Arizona high court had conceded that due process considerations had some relevance in juvenile court hearings, it found to be without merit the Gaults' complaints of deprivation of the rights to adequate notice of charges, to counsel, to confrontation and cross-examination of witnesses, to protection against self-incrimination, to a transcript of the hearing, and to an appeal.[25] For its decision, the Arizona Supreme Court relied upon the familiar argument that the juvenile court does "not exist to punish children for their transgressions" and "stands in the position of a protective parent rather than a prosecutor."[26]

The Gault case, while limited to proceedings to determine delinquency which might result in commitment to a state institution, gave the Supreme Court an opportunity to conduct a wide-ranging evaluation of what it called "a peculiar system for juveniles, unknown to our law in any comparable context."[27] It began its evaluation by casting a skeptical eye on the theory that juvenile court procedure could be justified by the theory of *parens patriae,* a phrase whose "meaning is murky" and whose "historical credentials are of dubious relevance."[28] Finding the "constitutional and theoretical basis for this peculiar system—to say the least—debatable,"[29] the Court has in *Gault* and in its subsequent decisions insisted upon looking past the "civil label-of-convenience"[30] to the actual distinctions, if any, between juvenile court processes and sanctions and criminal law processes and sanctions. Not willing to conclude that the processes were identical, the Court has not imported wholesale into juvenile court the safeguards available in criminal court. Instead, it has posed the question of which of these safeguards are "essentials of due process and fair treatment."[31]

There run through the decisions in *Kent, Gault, Winship, McKeiver,* and *Breed* both plaudits for the good intentions of the juvenile court reformers and laments for the disappointment of their high hopes. The decisions quote liberally from criticisms of the qualifications of juvenile court judges, the persisting incarceration of children with adults, rates of recidivism, the stigmatizing effect of delinquency findings, etc.[32] The gap between the real and the ideal juvenile court seems, then, to have played some role in these decisions. But as Justice Harlan pointed out in his concurrence in *Gault,*[33] it is not clear what the connection is between practical failings and constitutional validity. On the one hand, there is some reference to a *quid pro quo* which had promised rehabilitative treatment in exchange for procedural safeguards, and upon which the juvenile court had defaulted.[34] On the other hand, the fact about juvenile court hearings which seems most to have troubled the Supreme Court is one which juvenile court reformers never hoped to eliminate: the fact that those hearings might result in commitment to an institution, in loss of liberty.

Where, as the Supreme Court noted in *Gault,* early decisions of other courts had bolstered *parens patriae* doctrine by finding a right for children not to liberty but to custody, the Supreme Court decisions of the 1960's and 1970's have returned again and again to the deprivation of liberty which might result from juvenile court proceedings. They have insisted that incarceration, even in pursuit of a rehabilitative ideal, was too serious a consequence to reach without at least some control on judicial discretion. In *Gault* the Court expressed most forcefully its impatience with the euphemisms which concealed in juvenile court the issue of liberty. Justice Fortas wrote for the Court:

> It is of no constitutional significance—and of limited practical meaning—that the institution to which [the juvenile offender] is committed is called an Industrial School. The fact of the matter is that, however euphemistic the title, a "receiving home" or an "industrial school" for juveniles is an institution

of confinement in which the child is incarcerated for a greater or lesser time.[35]

In consequence of similarities it found between juvenile hearings which might result in commitment and criminal trials, the Supreme Court held that fundamental fairness in those hearings required notice of charges with adequate particularity and adequate time to prepare a defense; a right to be represented by counsel either privately retained or appointed by the court; the privilege against self-incrimination and, in the absence of a valid confession, the right to confront and cross-examine witnesses. The Court did not reach the question of a right to appellate review or to the provision of a transcript.

In re Winship raised the issue of the appropriate standard of proof in a proceeding to decide whether a child had committed an act which, if committed by an adult, would be a crime. Could a child be found delinquent for committing such an act upon "the preponderance of the evidence," the usual standard in civil cases, or did fair treatment require that such a decision rest upon proof beyond a reasonable doubt, the usual standard in criminal cases? The New York Court of Appeals, the state's highest court, had found the preponderance-of-the-evidence standard established by statute constitutionally valid. The United States Supreme Court disagreed, and again the possibility of incarceration was fundamental to its decision. Justice Brennan gave the majority's endorsement to the proposition that "a person accused of crime . . . would be at a severe disadvantage, a disadvantage amounting to a lack of fundamental fairness, if he could be adjudged guilty and imprisoned for years on the strength of the same evidence as would suffice in a civil case."[36] Justice Harlan explained in his concurring opinion that where, as in civil cases, only money damages between private parties are at stake, a lower standard of proof suffices. But where, as in juvenile court, essentially criminal sanctions might apply and liberty is at stake, the Constitution requires proof beyond a reasonable doubt.[37]

The theme of the essential similarity between the consequences of an adjudication of delinquency and of a criminal conviction carried through the case of *Breed v. Jones,* decided by the Supreme Court in 1974. The case involved a child who had first appeared in a California juvenile court which found truth in the allegations that the child had committed an act which, if committed by an adult, would have been the crime of armed robbery. At the separate dispositional hearing which followed, however, the same juvenile court had found the child unfit for treatment as a juvenile and had transferred him to a criminal court, where he was tried and convicted for the same offense and committed. His petition for a writ of *habeas corpus,* grounded on the claim that he had been twice put in jeopardy for the same offense in violation of the Fifth and Fourteenth Amendments, was unsuccessful in state courts. It failed as well in federal district court, but the Court of Appeals for the Ninth Circuit reversed, finding the protection against double jeopardy applied fully to this combination of a juvenile court adjudicative hearing and a criminal trial. The Supreme Court agreed. Since none of the lower courts had doubted that after transfer to criminal court the protection against double jeopardy applied to juveniles, or that the criminal conviction had placed the child in jeopardy for the same offense as had been before the juvenile court, the point at issue was whether the juvenile court proceeding had put the child in jeopardy at all in the constitutional sense. Chief Justice Burger wrote for a unanimous court: "It is too late in the day to conclude that a juvenile is not put in jeopardy at a proceeding whose object is to determine whether he has committed acts that violate a criminal law."[38] The stigma attached to findings of delinquency and, again, the possibility of incarceration—whether for punitive or for rehabilitative purposes—made juvenile court adjudicative hearings sufficiently similar to criminal trials to require the application of constitutional safeguards.[39]

Taken together, the three decisions in *Gault, Winship,* and *Breed* added many of those safeguards to juvenile court proceedings. In making these additions, the Supreme Court comforted itself and supporters of the juvenile court with the assertion that these safeguards would not interfere with those aspects of the juvenile court which still recommended themselves: the separation of juvenile from adult offenders, the confidentiality of juvenile court proceedings, the use of the label "delinquent" rather than of criminal labels, the search for individualized dispositions, and the absence of civil disabilities (like the loss of voting rights) which could attach to criminal convictions.[40]

From this list of virtues, informality of courtroom procedure is conspicuously absent. The Court recognized that the proponents of the juvenile court idea had hoped that, freed of procedural constraints, the juvenile court judge might approach the delinquent as parent or friend and thus help to effectuate his rehabilitation. In *Gault* the Court met this issue head on:

> . . . recent studies have, with surprising unanimity, entered a sharp dissent to this gentle conception. They suggest that the appearance as well as the actuality of fairness, impartiality and orderliness—in short, the essentials of due process may be a more impressive and therapeutic attitude so far as the juvenile is concerned.[41]

While it is difficult to see how the Court could pretend to preserve the essence of the juvenile court system while it chipped away at procedural informality, it is easy to see that in most of these cases it explicitly or implicitly rejected procedural informality as an acceptable or effective tool of rehabilitation. Only in *McKeiver* did the Court find the slightest virtue in procedural informality, and only in *McKeiver* did the Court fail to expand the meaning of due process for juveniles.

McKeiver et al. v. Pennsylvania raised the question whether a child accused in juvenile court of an act which would be a crime if committed by an adult had a right to trial by jury. Juvenile court reformers had considered trial by jury an unnecessary evil. The supreme court of Pennsylvania, in

rejecting McKeiver's claim, had considered jury trial potentially more disruptive to the juvenile court than any other
aspect of adversary procedure.[42] Taking advantage of the step-
by-step approach to due process estblished in *Gault,* the Supreme Court agreed that a right to trial by jury was not one of
those essentials of due process and fundamental fairness
which must be included in juvenile court.[43] In reaching this
conclusion, the Court distinguished the right to trial by jury
from those other rights which it had applied to the juvenile
courts: the rights to counsel, confrontation, and cross-examination of witnesses, and to the standard of proof beyond a
reasonable doubt, it said, all related to improving the fact-
finding capacity of a court; the jury trial did not.[44] Finally,
the Court clung to its earlier reassurances that the thrust of its
decisions was not to do away with the juvenile court system
entirely: it rejected McKeiver's claim because it was possible
that jury trials "will make the juvenile process into a fully
adversary process and will put an effective end to what has
been the idealistic prospect of an intimate, informal, protective proceeding."[45] In contrast to its position in other decisions, the Court in *McKeiver* seems to have believed that it
was facing a challenge which, if won, would deny the juvenile court its reason for a separate existence. "Perhaps," wrote
Justice Blackmun for the majority, "that ultimate disillusion-
ment will come one day, but for the moment we are disinclined to give impetus to it."[46]

The decision in *McKeiver* indicated that the Court had
some attachment to the residuum of informality in juvenile
court, although it defended its attachment not so much by
investing that residuum with virtue of its own as by making it
seem indispensable to the continued existence of the juvenile
court. The decision also indicated that the choice of a piece-
meal approach to due process in juvenile court had practical
consequences. Given the many issues remaining to be decided
in all stages of juvenile court procedure, it may well have
practical consequences again. But the point here is not to
predict what will happen in the future; nor is it merely to
detail the ways in which the Supreme Court has domesticated

juvenile justice in the past. It is to suggest that the application of due process thinking reveals the weakening hold of the ideas which motivated the creation of the juvenile court.

Most directly and obviously, the application of due process thinking to the juvenile court indicated the reemergence in a somewhat different guise of opposition to judicial discretion, an opposition which had once bolstered the appeal of classical criminology and penology. As the Supreme Court said in *Gault,* "Juvenile Court history has again demonstrated that unbridled discretion, however benevolently motivated, is frequently a poor substitute for principle and procedure."[47] It was particularly clear in *Gault* that the Supreme Court did not trust the state acting through the juvenile court to serve the interests of the child while it pursued the interests of the community. About the need for representation by counsel, the Court said: "The probation officer cannot act as counsel for the child. His role in the adjudicatory hearing is, by statute and in fact, as arresting officer and witness against the child. Nor can the judge represent the child."[48] About the privilege against self-incrimination, the Court said: "One of its purposes is to prevent the state, whether by force or by psychological domination, from overcoming the mind and will of the person under investigation and depriving him of the freedom to decide whether to assist the state in securing his conviction."[49] Given the progressive faith in the state's benevolent exercise of its discretion, this wariness of the state acting through its judicial arm in juvenile court signified considerable change. But stating the issue simply in terms of judicial discretion and power combines a number of issues which deserve attention separately.

The purpose of eliminating counsel, jury, certain rules of evidence and standards of proof, and other aspects of adversary procedure from juvenile court was not to increase judicial discretion as an end in itself. The purpose was to deemphasize questions of guilt and innocence of specific acts so that the judge might hear information pertaining to a general state of delinquency, information which would help him exercise discretion in ways responsive to the insights of science and the needs of particular children. By introducing elements of adversary process, according to the opinion in *McKeiver,* the Supreme Court intended to improve the fact-finding capacity of the juvenile court. The Court evidently shared the conclusion expressed by the President's Commission on Law Enforcement that

> . . . efforts to help and heal and treat, if they are to have any chance of success, must be based upon accurate determination of facts—the facts of the conduct that led to the filing of the petition and also the facts of the child's past conduct and relationships. The essential attributes of the judicial trial are the best guarantee our system has been able to devise for assuring reliable determination of fact.[50]

This conclusion rejected the progressive faith in informal techniques for information gathering. It also reasserted the importance of a particular sort of information—information which bears on the question of guilt or innocence; the kind of facts which a lawyer elicits in cross-examination and which must be proven beyond a reasonable doubt to sustain an order of incarceration; the kind of facts which juvenile court reformers considered not only less important than the "social" facts of a child's environment but an obstacle to finding the social facts.

It is not clear whether the Supreme Court or the commission shared the reformers' opinion that the two kinds of facts compete with each other, or therefore, whether by their emphasis on the facts of guilt or innocence they intended to drive the social facts out of the juvenile court. Neither, however, seems likely. Rather, it seems that they considered facts of guilt or innocence the first and indispensable kind for the adjudicative hearing, and facts of the social kind important, if at all, to dispositional questions. That social facts took second place sequentially and in importance had something to do with the increased value attached to liberty and the decreased confidence in the benevolence of the state. It had also to do with a loss of faith in the sciences upon which the interpretation of social facts depends.

The evidence for the decline of faith in scientific approaches to delinquency is largely indirect in the cases we have discussed, but it is there. *McKeiver,* ironically the only one of these cases which turned back a due process challenge, gives the best direct evidence. The opinion in *McKeiver* quoted liberally from the Task Force Report on Juvenile Delinquency and Youth Crime, which constituted part of the product of the President's Commission on Law Enforcement and the Administration of Justice. In particular, it quoted the Task Force as attributing disaffection with the juvenile court to the following factors: "the community's unwillingness to provide people and facilities and to be concerned, the insufficiency of time devoted, the scarcity of professional help, the inadequacy of dispositional alternatives, and *our general lack of knowledge* [emphasis mine]."[51] It also quoted the Task Force as attributing the persistence of punitive elements in juvenile court, in spite of the rehabilitative ideal, "not only . . . [to] the absence of facilities and personnel but also . . . [to] the limits of knowledge and technique."[52]

One finds clearer evidence of a loss of faith in scientific answers to the problem of delinquency outside the Supreme Court. In 1954, a Children's Bureau publication about delinquency prevention programs asked: "What . . . [do we know] about how to prevent or reduce delinquency?" and answered, "With certainty, rather little."[53] The study's conclusion that "we are on our way toward learning what does and does not prevent delinquency, but . . . still have far to go"[54] was rather more generous than others have been. In an influential essay first published in 1959, Professor Francis A. Allen warned that to base power upon knowledge which does not exist is to invite the abuse of power.

> . . . The values of individual liberty may be imperiled by claims to knowledge and therapeutic technique that we in fact do not possess and by failure candidly to concede what we do not know. . . . Ignorance, in itself, is not disgraceful so long as it is unavoidable. But when we rush to measures affecting human liberty and human dignity on the assump-

tion that we know what we do not know or can do what we
cannot do, then the problem of ignorance takes on a more
sinister hue.[55]

The problem of the juvenile court was not, as another article
in 1959 expressed it, either power alone or ignorance alone:
the dilemma was that the juvenile court had "too much power
with too little knowledge."[56] These writers aimed not to discredit the rehabilitative ideal but to adjust practice to the fact
that the ideal hovered over an ever-receding horizon. In 1976,
that horizon seemed no nearer: two legal scholars wrote that
"there is little reason to believe that any effective way to
reduce recidivism through coercive rehabilitation has been
found."[57]

Thus, the opposition to unbridled discretion in juvenile
court was made of several parts: a high value placed on
liberty, a low opinion of the government's trustworthiness
where individual liberty is at stake, a distrust of administrative
decision-making, and a skepticism about the capacity of the
social sciences to teach us very much of practical use about
the causes and cures of deviant behavior. The parts added up
in the decisions of the Supreme Court to a position which one
might call moderately noninterventionist: due process gave
children in juvenile court a new line of defense against the
state intervention which follows a finding of delinquency.
The Court's position resembled that of the commission report
from which it so liberally quoted, a position which Michael
Tonry has described as containing a "fatalistic prognosis that
the best we can do is stumble along as before but hopefully—
by diversion, due process and deinstitutionalization—cause
less harm to fewer children."[58] The main reason left, both for
the Court and for the commission, to preserve the juvenile
court system in some form was that the criminal justice system
was worse.[59]

From the distrust of power without knowledge, other
opinion radiated into areas which the Court had not yet
touched. In one lay the hallowed ground of individualized
justice. A report on crime and punishment prepared for the

American Friends Service Committee in 1971 concluded that not only judicial discretion in adjudication but judicial discretion in disposition should be reined in, and that the law should return to fitting the punishment to the crime rather than the criminal.[60] The agnostics' call for a return to the notion of "just deserts,"[61] was joined by those who considered positivist criminology and individualized justice not only unproven but fundamentally wrong.[62]

Demands for more restricted and fixed dispositions had a parallel in demands for a narrower definition of delinquency. The definition which included noncriminal behavior appealed to the early reformers because it had preventive implications and because, we have hypothesized, it discouraged behavior which was in itself objectionable to them. Lack of proof of a connection between noncriminal and criminal behavior has called the first justification into question; accusations of class bias have called the second into question. By due process standards the noncriminal jurisdiction appears too vague to give young people adequate notice of what behavior it prohibits. Labeling theory, if it advises against official handling in delinquency cases generally, applies *a fortiori* against including unnecessary classes of conduct among those which may trigger court action. Most of these considerations influenced the President's Commission on Law Enforcement to recommend that serious consideration be given to eliminating noncriminal conduct altogether from the juvenile court laws.[63] A final argument for narrower jurisdiction bears scrutiny because it fans out to cover many issues in juvenile justice, and to characterize well the attitude toward that system in the second half of the twentieth century.

As the Supreme Court noted in *Gault,* the juvenile court laws as presently enforced reach many, many young people; if perfectly enforced they could reach as many as 90 percent of the juvenile population, so widespread is the behavior they seek to control.[64] Even in a world of unlimited legal resources —of courts and judges and probation officers without number—law that made punishable behavior which was engaged in by the vast majority of the population would be law of questionable legitimacy and wisdom. Ours is not a world of unlimited legal resources; still less is it a world of unlimited rehabilitative resources. In such a world it is wise to realize that the law is a tool for *making* criminals and delinquents, as well as for sanctioning them; we can use it sparingly or wantonly as we choose. Wheeler and Cottrell estimate that some 25 percent of the cases handled by juvenile courts involve acts which, like incorrigibility and curfew violations, do not violate the criminal law.[65] If the courts and their probation staffs are overburdened, the argument goes, eliminating noncriminal "offenses" from their agenda offers one sensible way to relieve them.[66] Retaining noncriminal jurisdiction and expending limited legal resources in the effort to control proto-criminal behavior might make sense if such behavior were demonstrably linked to a future of serious crime, and if those resources were demonstrably effective in severing that link. In the late twentieth century, neither demonstration seems possible. On the contrary, one could more easily demonstrate that "underlying these difficulties with the proto-criminal norms of the juvenile law is the more fundamental problem that law is a grossly inadequate device for achieving positive socialization."[67] To continue using an inadequate device on unnecessary tasks when it is needed for others is wasteful.

This argument does not stop at getting back to basics in the definition of delinquency: its force goes beyond details to recommend a return to essentials in the juvenile justice system generally. Friends and foes alike of the rehabilitative ideal can agree that the essential function of the juvenile justice system, like that of the criminal justice system, lies in the effort—however frustrating—to control behavior which truly disrupts and threatens social life. Not only courts and judges, probation officers and prisons are necessary to that effort. It also requires the moral capital of the state, a limited resource that ought not to be frittered away in attempts to do the impossible and inessential in full public view. The consensus grows that the juvenile court has attempted—particularly in the effort to fuse true justice with true compassion—the impossible, if not the undesirable.

It is ironic that the typically progressive concern for rational conservation of resources should come to constrain the typically progressive ambition to solve social problems through a marriage of science and law. The impact of this renewed modesty is not, in any event, likely to eliminate the juvenile court from the juvenile justice system. Truly radical noninterventionism, based on the conviction that most delinquents will grow out of their delinquency if only we leave them alone,[68] has too much opposition from people who call for greater certainty and severity of punishment. The noninterventionists may succeed in narrowing the definition of delinquency toward the core of criminal behavior, thus limiting the juvenile court's preventive ambitions. The law-and-order contingent may succeed in restricting the use of probation and other forms of flexibility in treating delinquents, thus limiting the court's rehabilitative pretensions. These changes, added to the considerable success of the due process critics, would leave the juvenile court a very different institution from the one envisaged by progressive reformers. But the juvenile court will survive in some form if only because treatment of child offenders separately from adult offenders seems harmless, and because a society does not easily drop from its repertory old ways of facing social problems.

Still, if the change in our understanding of delinquency and how to deal with it is not total, it is nevertheless significant. All the changes in the juvenile court which have already occurred, and virtually all of those which may occur, confess directly or indirectly the belief that we do not know what to do about juvenile crime, and a fear that collectively we can do nothing. This seems true even of the demands for harder sanctions: they represent more a desire to find symbols of community outrage than to advocate a strategy with any promise of success.

The sense of helplessness in the face of juvenile crime is one sign among many that the promises of modern society are not being kept. Neither experience nor theory has been kind to assumptions of the innocence of childhood, the malleability of human behavior, the competence of science, the efficiency or benevolence of the state. These assumptions carried us to a high plateau of intervention and left us exposed to serious disappointment; from this position of exposure, due process thinking and more modest ambitions may help us stage a not too undignified retreat. We need not be too gloomy about the retreat: if experience dictates that we aim to do less with law, there is at least the possible satisfaction of doing it more frankly and fairly.

NOTES

Abbreviations

Procs. of NCSW: Proceedings of the National Conference of Social Work
Procs. of NCCC: Proceedings of the National Conference of Charities and
    Correction
Annals: Annals of the American Academy of Political and Social Science
Yearbook of NPA: Yearbook of the National Probation Association

Introduction

1. These positions are associated respectively with Richard Hofstadter, *The Age of Reform* (New York, 1955); Robert H.
   Wiebe, *The Search for Order 1887–1920* (New York, 1967);
   Gabriel Kolko, *The Triumph of Conservatism* (New York, 1963).
2. The "semantic" problem is raised by David M. Kennedy, ed., in
   his historiographical introduction to *Progressivism: The Critical
   Issues* (Boston, 1971), p. xii.
3. P. 176.
4. *From the Depths: The Discovery of Poverty in the United States*
   (New York, 1965), p. 15.
5. Foster Rhea Dulles, *Labor in America* (New York, 2nd rev. ed.,
   1960), p. 171.
6. James Penick, Jr., "The Progressives and the Environment: Three
   Themes from the First Conservation Movement," in *The Progressive Era*, ed. Lewis Gould (Syracuse, N.Y., 1974), p. 117.
7. See, for example, Samuel Hays, "The Politics of Reform in
   Municipal Government," *Pacific Northwest Quarterly*, LV
   (October 1964), pp. 157–69; Thomas K. McGraw, "The Progressive Legacy," in *The Progressive Era*, p. 200.

8. "Urban Reform," in *The Progressive Era*, pp. 133–52.
9. *Conservation and the Gospel of Efficiency* (Cambridge, Mass., 1959).
   See also Hays, *Response to Industrialism 1885–1914* (Chicago, 1957), pp. 156–58.
10. R. Laurence Moore, "Directions of Thought in the Progressive Era," in *The Progressive Era*, p. 36.
11. David M. Kennedy, *Progressivism: The Critical Issues,* p. viii.
12. *Modernization: The Transformation of American Life 1600–1865* (New York, 1976), particularly pp. 3–22.

1. Origins of the Juvenile Court

1. Quoted in Joseph M. Hawes, *Children in Urban Society: Juvenile Delinquency in Nineteenth Century America* (New York, 1971), p. 28.
2. Chief George Matsell, quoted in Robert M. Mennel, *Thorns and Thistles: Juvenile Delinquents in the United States, 1825–1940* (Hanover, N.H., 1973), p. 31.
3. Quoted in Bremner, op. cit., p. 213.
4. "New York Children's Court," *Juvenile Record* III, No. 2 (February 1902), p. 7.
5. Burdette Lewis, *The Offender and His Relations to Law and Society* (New York, 1917), pp. 22–23.
6. E. H. Sutherland, "Criminology, Public Opinion and the Law," *Procs of NCSW*, LIV (1927), 171.
7. Stephen Schlossman, *Love and the American Delinquent: The Theory and Practice of "Progressive" Juvenile Justice, 1825–1920* (Chicago, 1977), pp. 18, 33–34, 38.
8. Henry Wood, "The Psychology of Crime," *The Arena*, 8:529 (October 1893), p. 531.
9. A. R. Whiteway, *Recent Object-Lessons in Penal Science* (New York, 1902), pp. 17–18.
10. Thomas Travis, *Young Malefactors: A Study in Juvenile Delinquency, Its Causes and Treatment* (New York, 1908), p. 187.
11. Nathan Oppenheim, *The Development of the Child* (New York, 1898), p. 4.
12. Ibid., p. 206.
13. *Crime, Its Causes and Treatment* (New York, 1922), p. 273.
14. *Delinquency and Drift* (New York, 1964), p. 6.
15. Ibid., p. 7.
16. M. P. E. Grossman, "Criminality in Children," *The Arena*, 22 (Oct.–Nov. 1899), p. 645.
17. *Juvenile Offenders* (New York, 1897), p. 31.

18. *The Spirit of Social Work* (New York, 1912), p. 111.
19. Op. cit., p. 169.
20. P. 52.
21. P. 97.
22. Frederick Tracy, *The Psychology of Childhood* (Boston, 1909), p. 187.
23. "The Contents of Children's Minds on Entering School," *Pedagogical Seminary* I (June 1891), pp. 139–73.
24. "Recent Progress in the Juvenile Court Movement," *Procs. of NCCC,* XXXI (1904), pp. 250–57.
25. Anthony Platt, *The Child-Savers* (Chicago, 1969), p. 107.
26. Quoted in Thurston, op. cit., p. 84.
27. Platt, op. cit., pp. 117, 183–202.

2. The Ideal Juvenile Court

1. Laws of Colorado (1903), chap. 94.
2. From a discussion reported in *Procs. of NCCC,* XXXI (1904), p. 632.
3. Grace Abbott, "Topical Abstract of Juvenile Court Laws," in *Juvenile Court Laws in the United States Summarized,* ed. Hastings H. Hart (New York, 1910), p. 129.
4. Benjamin Lindsey, *The Problem of the Child and How Colorado Cares for Him* (Denver, 1904), pp. 47–48.
5. "The Reformation of Juvenile Delinquents through the Juvenile Court," *Procs. of NCCC,* XXX (1903), p. 213.
6. Op. cit.
7. *Our Penal Machinery and Its Victims* (Chicago, 1884), p. 47.
8. A. L. Jacoby, M.D., "The New Approach to the Problem of Delinquency: Punishment vs. Treatment," *Procs. of NCSW,* LIII (1926), p. 179.
9. Ruth Workum, "The Relation Between Functions of the Juvenile Court and Those of General Child-Rearing Agencies," *Procs. of NCSW,* XLIX (1922), p. 144.
10. "The Juvenile Court," *Report of the American Bar Association,* XXXIV (1909), p. 470.
11. Evelina Belden, *Courts in the United States Hearing Children's Cases,* U.S. Children's Bureau Publication #65 (Washington, D.C., 1920), p. 8.
12. *Manual for Probation Officers in New York* (Albany, 1918), p. 58.
13. Op. cit., p. 126.
14. Introduction to Sophonsiba Breckenridge, *The Delinquent Child and the Home* (New York, 1912), pp. 2–4.

15. Ibid.
16. Op. cit., pp. 135, 139.
17. Op. cit., pp. 57, 62.
18. From a discussion reported in *Procs. of NCCC*, XXIX (1902), p. 425.
19. Arthur MacDonald, *Abnormal Man* (Washington, D.C., 1893), p. 53.
20. "Remedial Work on Behalf of our Youth," *Procs. of NCCC*, XXII (1895), p. 237.
21. *Progressivism and the Slums: Tenement House Reform in New York City 1890–1917* (Pittsburgh, 1962), pp. 2, 7.
22. David M. Kennedy, *Birth Control in America: The Career of Margaret Sanger* (New Haven, 1970), p. 15.
23. Ibid.
24. Mack, op. cit., p. 465.
25. Reverend Malcolm Dana, op. cit., p. 237.
26. Mary E. McDowell, "Friendly Visiting," *Procs. of NCCC*, XXIII (1896), p. 253.
27. "One Day in Juvenile Court," *Juvenile Court Record*, II, No. 1 (1900), quoted in his *Concerning Delinquency: Progressive Changes in Our Perspectives* (New York, 1942), p. 95.
28. Op. cit., p. 24.
29. Ibid., p. 69.
30. Ibid., p. 69–78.
31. J. J. Kelso, "Reforming Delinquent Children," *Procs. of NCCC*, XXX (1903), p. 231.
32. *The Problem of the Child*, p. 35.
33. From the speech of Lebeziatnikov to Rodya, p. 365 of the Bantam paperback edition of Feodor Dostoevsky's *Crime and Punishment*.
34. E. E. York, "The Cultivation of Individuality," *Procs. of NCCC*, XXIX (1902), p. 262.
35. MacDonald, op. cit., p. 53.
36. Timothy D. Hurley, "Juvenile Probation," *Procs. of NCCC*, XXXIV (1907), p. 225.
37. Henry Thurston, "Third Day in Juvenile Court" (1900), in *Concerning Delinquency*, p. 99.
38. Robert Baldwin, quoted in Hastings H. Hart, *Preventive Treatment of Neglected Children* (New York, 1910), p. 272.
39. Homer Folks, "Juvenile Probation," *Procs. of NCCC*, XXXII (1906), p. 118.
40. Walter Wheeler in discussion, *Procs. of NCCC*, XXXI (1904), p. 570.
41. "The Jurisprudence of Juvenile Deviance," in Margaret Rosenheim, ed., *Pursuing Justice for the Child* (Chicago, 1976), p. 8.

42. Op. cit., p. 150.
43. *The Borderland of Criminal Justice: Essays in Law and Criminology* (Chicago, 1964), p. 46.
44. Schlossman, op. cit., p. 66.

3. *The Legal Setting*

1. "Two Models of the Criminal Process," *U. of Pennsylvania Law Review* 113:1 (1964), pp. 1–68.
2. *Powell v. Alabama* 287 U.S. 45 (1932).
3. Ibid., at 53.
4. Ibid., at 76.
5. Anthony Lewis, *Gideon's Trumpet* (New York, 1964), p. 108.
6. *Betts v. Brady* 316 U.S. 455, 471.
7. 372 U.S. 335 (1963).
8. *In Re Gault* 387 U.S. 1 (1967).
9. Richard M. Brown, "Legal and Behavioral Perspectives on American Vigilantism," in *Perspectives in American History*, V (1971), pp. 96–144.
10. Pound treats these matters both in "The Causes of Popular Dissatisfaction with the Administration of Justice," in *Reports of the American Bar Association* 29 (1906), pp. 395–417, and in *Criminal Justice in America* (New York, 1930).
11. Quoted in Brown, "Legal and Behavioral Perspectives," p. 136.
12. *The Common Law* (Boston, 1881), p. 41.
13. "The Juvenile Court, Its Legal Aspects," in *Annals of the American Academy of Political and Social Sciences* XXXVI, No. 1 (July 1910), pp. 49–50.
14. "Theory and Practice of the Juvenile Court," in *Procs. of NCCC*, XXXI (1904), p. 364.
15. Schlossman, op. cit., p. 13; Hawes, op. cit., pp. 46–47.
16. *Ex Parte Crouse* 4 Wharton (Pa.) 9 (1838).
17. Flexner and Reuben Oppenheimer, *Legal Aspect of the Juvenile Court,* U.S. Children's Bureau Publication No. 99 (Washington, D.C., 1922), p. 7.
18. Quoted in Margaret Rosenheim, ed., *Justice for the Child: The Juvenile Court in Transition* (New York, 1962), p. 2.
19. Herbert Lou, *Juvenile Courts in the United States* (Chapel Hill, 1927), p. 5.
20. 151 Mich. 315 (1908).
21. 213 Pa. 48 (1905).
22. Ibid., at 56, 54.
23. 15 Idaho 120 (1908), at 129–30.
24. *Commonwealth v. Fisher* 213 Pa. 48, at 53.

25. *Kent Mercein v. The People ex. rel. Barry,* 25 Wendell (N.Y.)
    64 (1840); *Ex Parte Crouse* 4 Wharton (Pa.) 9 (1847).
26. 119 Cal. 496 (1897).
27. Lou, op. cit., p. 9.
28. *Application of Gault* 99 Ariz. 181 (1965).
29. 31 Utah 473 (1907).
30. "Abolish the 'Insanity Defense'— Why Not?," in Abraham Gold-
    stein and Joseph Goldstein, eds., *Crime, Law and Society* (New
    York, 1971), p. 416.
31. Ibid., p. 417.
32. *Procs. of NCCC,* XXIX (1902), pp. 449–50.
33. Katz and Goldstein, op. cit., p. 419.
34. In *Crime and Delinquency,* Vol. 19, No. 4 (October 1973),
    pp. 457–76.

4. *The Ideal in Practice*

1. Emily E. Williamson, "Probation and the Juvenile Courts,"
   Annals, Vol. 20 (1902), p. 259.
2. George W. Stubbs, "The Mission of the Juvenile Court," *Procs.
   of NCCC,* XXXI (1904), pp. 352–53.
3. "Recent Progress of the Juvenile Court Movement," p. 166; "The
   Reformation of Delinquents through the Juvenile Court," p. 212.
4. Belden, op. cit., p. 10.
5. "Juvenile Detention Homes," *Yearbook of NPA* (1925), pp.
   92–93.
6. *Proceedings of the Conference on Juvenile Court Standards,*
   U.S. Children's Bureau Publication No. 97 (Washington, D.C.,
   1922).
7. William I. Thomas, *The Child in America: Behavior Problems
   and Programs* (New York, 1928), p. 135.
8. Katherine Lenroot and Emma Lundberg, *Juvenile Courts at
   Work,* U.S. Children's Bureau Publication No. 141 (Washington, D.C., 1925), p. 94. The study focused on juvenile courts in
   Buffalo, Boston, Denver, Washington, D.C., Los Angeles, Min-
   neapolis, New Orleans, San Francisco, Seattle, and St. Louis.
9. Emma Lundberg, "The Juvenile Court as a Constructive Social
   Agency," *Procs. of NCSW,* XLIX (1922), p. 155.
10. George Mangold, *Problems of Child Welfare* (New York, 1914),
    p. 366.
11. *Report of the New York State Probation Commission* (Albany,
    1906), pp. 28–29.
12. P. 41.
13. "The Juvenile Court: Its Uses and Limitations," *Procs. of the
    American Prison Congress* (1906), p. 249.

14. *The Juvenile Court and the Community* (New York, 1914), pp. 45–46.
15. "The Evolution of the Juvenile Court," *Annals*, CV (January 23, 1923), pp. 219–20.
16. "How to Study a Case of Delinquency," *Procs. of NCSW*, XLVIII (1926), p. 85.
17. Pp. 46–47.
18. P. 55.
19. P. 172.
20. P. 188.
21. Thomas, op. cit., p. 121.
22. *Delinquents and Criminals: Their Making and Unmaking* (New York, 1926), p. 64.
23. Belle Boone Beard, *Juvenile Probation* (New York, 1934), pp. 147–48.
24. P. 233.
25. "The Close of Another Chapter in Criminology," *Mental Hygiene*, XIX, No. 2 (April 1935), pp. 208–22.
26. Lenroot, "The Evolution of the Juvenile Court," p. 218.
27. Helen Rankin Jeter, *The Chicago Juvenile Court*, U.S. Children's Bureau Publication No. 104 (Washington, D.C., 1922), pp. 42–43.
28. In *Annals*, Vol. 145 (September–November 1929), p. 90.
29. C. C. Carstens, "The Contribution of the Juvenile Court to the Child Welfare Movement," from *Procs. of the Conference on Juvenile Court Standards*, U.S. Children's Bureau Publication No. 97 (Washington, D.C., 1922), p. 12; *Juvenile Court Standards*, pp. 26–27; Charles L. Chute, "The Needs and Future of the Probation Service," in *Procs. of NCSW*, XLIX (1922), p. 175.
30. Henry S. Hulbert, "Probation," in *The Child, the Clinic and the Court*, ed. Jane Addams (New York, 1925), p. 238.
31. Lenroot, quoted in Hulbert, op. cit., pp. 238–39.
32. Charles L. Chute, "The Crime Wave and Probation," *Journal of Criminal Law and Criminology*, XII, No. 3 (1921), p. 418.
33. Francis H. Hiller, "The Juvenile Court as a Case-Working Agency: Its Limitations and Its Possibilities," *Procs. of NCSW*, LII (1926), p. 144.
34. Bernard Glueck, M.D., "Psychiatric Treatment and Probation," *Yearbook of NPA* (1923), pp. 57–58.
35. Thomas, op. cit., p. 143.
36. "Knowing Your Individual," *Yearbook of NPA* (1923), p. 230.
37. Harry R. Archbald, "The Youth of Today from the Judicial Standpoint," *Yearbook of NPA* (1924), p. 299.
38. Op. cit., p. 461.

39. *Juvenile Court Standards,* Report of the Committee of the Children's Bureau (Washington, D.C., 1923), p. 58.

5. *Psychology*

1. Hawes, op. cit., p. 190.
2. P. 207.
3. Platt, op. cit., p. 44.
4. *The Professional Altruist: The Emergence of Social Work as a Career* (Cambridge, Mass., 1965), p. 16.
5. P. 38.
6. Op. cit., p. 3.
7. Lubove, op. cit., p. 109.
8. Virginia Robinson, *A Changing Psychology in Social Casework* (Chapel Hill, 1930), pp. 28, 53.
9. *Social Work* (New York, 1922), p. 17.
10. Jesse Taft, "Early Conditioning of Personality in the Pre-School Child," *School and Society,* XXI, No. 546 (June 13, 1925), p. 690.
11. Porter Lee and Marion Kenworthy, *Mental Hygiene and Social Work* (New York, 1929), p. 237.
12. Ibid., pp. 229–30.
13. *Youth in Conflict* (New York, 1925), p. 1.
14. Robinson, op. cit., pp. 18–20.
15. H. H. Goddard, "In the light of recent developments, what should be our policy in dealing with the delinquents, juvenile and adult?" *Journal of Criminal Law and Criminology,* XI, No. 3 (November 1920), p. 247.
16. Joseph Jastrow, "Psychology and Crime," *Procs. of NCSW,* LIV (1927), p. 163.
17. "Psychiatric Treatment and Probation," p. 61.
18. "The Psychic Factors in Juvenile Delinquency," *Mental Hygiene,* XI, No. 4 (October 1927), p. 764.
19. "Knowing Your Individual," p. 228.
20. Healy and Bonner, *Delinquents and Criminals,* pp. 106–60.
21. "Childhood: The Golden Period for Mental Hygiene," *Mental Hygiene,* IV, No. 2 (April 1920), p. 261.
22. *Concerning Delinquency,* p. 123.
23. "The Close of Another Chapter in Criminology," p. 217.
24. "Psychiatric Aims in the Field of Criminology," *Mental Hygiene,* II, No. 4 (October 1918), p. 548.
25. Op. cit., p. 85.
26. "Modifying Human Conduct," *Yearbook of NPA* (1929), p. 209.
27. Ibid., pp. 208–9.

28. Quoted in Hendrik M. Ruitenbeek, *Freud and America* (New York, 1966), p. 74.
29. Sigmund Freud, *An Outline of Psychoanalysis* (New York, 1949), p. 20.
30. Ibid., p. 110.
31. Reprinted in Richard Korn, ed., *Juvenile Delinquency* (New York, 1968), p. 35.
32. Ibid., p. 14.
33. Quoted in Hawes, op. cit., p. 196.
34. *Juvenile Delinquency* (New York, 1921), pp. 6–7.
35. Cyril Burt, *The Young Delinquent* (New York, 1933), p. 587.
36. Op. cit., pp. 159–60.
37. Freud, op. cit., pp. 104–5.
38. Lubove, op. cit., p. 87.
39. Ibid., p. 77.
40. "The Influence of Psychiatry on Social Work," reprinted in Fern Lowry, ed., *Readings in Social Casework* (New York, 1939), p. 695.
41. "The Relationship of the Psychiatric Clinic to the Juvenile Court," *Mental Hygiene*, XIII, No. 4 (October 1929), p. 715.
42. "The Rational Treatment of Juvenile Delinquency," *Yearbook of NPA* (1928), p. 369.
43. Lubove, op. cit., p. 99.
44. Quoted in Hawes, op. cit., p. 249.
45. Op. cit., p. 131.
46. Selection from *Children Who Hate*, reprinted in Korn, op. cit., pp. 133, 135.

6. Sociology

1. *New Light on Juvenile Delinquency and Its Treatment* (New Haven, 1936).
2. *Delinquent Boys: The Culture of the Gang* (New York, copyright 1955, pbk. edition, 1971), pp. 13–14.
3. Ibid., pp. 32–33.
4. Ibid., p. 18.
5. Ibid., p. 30.
6. "Lower-Class Culture as a Delinquency Generating Milieu," *The Journal of Social Issues*, XIV (1958), p. 19.
7. Cohen, op. cit., p. 129.
8. Ibid., p. 28.
9. Ibid., pp. 130–31.
10. Ibid., pp. 25–26.

11. Gresham M. Sykes and David Matza, "Techniques of Neutralization: A Theory of Delinquency," *The American Journal of Sociology*, XXII (December 1957), pp. 64–65.

12. "Social Structure and Anomie," in *American Sociological Review*, III (October 1938), p. 674.

13. Ibid., p. 682.

14. Op. cit., *The American Journal of Sociology*, XXII (December 1957), pp. 664–70.

15. *Delinquency and Drift*, p. 101.

16. "Juvenile Courts: Quest and Realities," *Juvenile Delinquency and Youth Crime*, Task Force Report, p. 94.

17. Matza, *Delinquency and Drift*, p. 97.

18. Ibid.

19. *Juvenile Delinquency: Its Prevention and Control* (New York, 1966), p. 33.

20. *The Challenge of Crime in a Free Society* (Washington, D.C., 1967), p. 85.

Conclusion

1. Bernard Flexner, "A Decade of the Juvenile Court," *Procs. of NCCC*, XXXVII (1910), p. 116.

2. "My Lesson from the Juvenile Court," *Survey* (February 5, 1910), p. 652.

3. Op. cit.

4. Introduction to *Proceedings of the Conference on Juvenile Court Standards*, U.S. Children's Bureau Publication No. 97 (Washington, D.C., 1922), pp. 8–9.

5. "The Delinquent Attitude—A Study of Juvenile Delinquents from the Standpoint of Human Relationships," *Procs. of NCSW*, LI (1924), p. 165.

6. "Mental Attitudes of Adults in a Juvenile Court," *Yearbook of NPA* (1929), pp. 141–42.

7. Paula Clare in discussion, *Yearbook of NPA* (1929), p. 204.

8. Grace Abbott, *The Child and the State* (Chicago, 1938), pp. 334–35.

9. "The Court and the Delinquent Child," in *American Journal of Sociology*, XXVI, No. 2 (September 1920), p. 178.

10. Thomas D. Eliot, "The Unofficial Treatment of Quasi-Delinquent Children," *Yearbook of NPA* (1922), p. 102.

11. "The Passing of the Juvenile Court," *Survey* (February 1921), p. 705.

12. "The Court and the Delinquent Child," pp. 179–80.

13. *Journal of Criminal Law and Criminology*, XII (1922), p. 339.

14. Murphy, op. cit., p. 88.
15. L. Guy Brown, "Social Causes and Cures for Delinquency," *Yearbook of NPA* (1930), p. 25.
16. Comment on Section 8.
17. Section 712(a)(b).
18. Children's Bureau Statistical Series No. 85, *Juvenile Court Statistics: 1965* (Washington, D.C., 1966), pp. 1–3.
19. See, for example, Report of the President's Commission on Law Enforcement and the Administration of Justice, *The Challenge of Crime in a Free Society* (Washington, D.C., 1967); Report of the President's Commission on Crime in the District of Columbia (Washington, D.C., 1966); McCune, *Profile of the Nation's Juvenile Court Judges* (Washington, D.C., 1965); Wheeler and Cottrell, op. cit.; Margaret Rosenheim, ed., *Justice for the Child.*
20. P. 80.
21. Ibid.
22. Ibid., p. 81.
23. See, for example, J. Lawrence Schultz and Fred Cohen, "Isolationism in Juvenile Court Jurisprudence," in *Pursuing Justice for the Child,* pp. 20–42.
24. 383 *U.S.* 541 (1966), at 555.
25. *Application of Gault* 99 Ariz. 181 (1965).
26. Ibid., at 188.
27. *In re Gault* 387 U.S. 1 (1967), at 17.
28. Ibid., at 16.
29. Ibid., at 17.
30. Ibid., at 50.
31. The formulation first appears in *Kent* 383 U.S., at 562; it is repeated in *Gault* 387 U.S., at 30; *In re Winship* 397 U.S. 358 (1969), at 359; *McKeiver et al., v. Pennsylvania* 403 U.S. 528 (1971), at 534.
32. *Kent v. U.S.* 383 U.S., at 555–56; *In re Gault* 387 U.S., at 17–19, 50, notes 14, 23, 31; *In re Winship* 397 U.S., at 363; *McKeiver et al. v. Pennsylvania* 403 U.S., at 534, note 5; *Breed v. Jones* 421 U.S. 519 (1975), at 528.
33. 387 U.S., at 66–67.
34. *Kent v. U.S.* 383 U.S., at 555–56; *In re Gault* 387 U.S., at note 30.
35. 387 U.S., at 27.
36. 397 U.S., at 363, quoting the dissenting opinion to the decision of the New York Court of Appeals.
37. Ibid., at 371–74.
38. *Breed, Director California Youth Authority v. Jones* 421 U.S. 519 (1975), at 529.
39. 421 U.S., at 530.

40. *In re Gault* 387 U.S., at 22–25; *In re Winship* 397 U.S., at 366.
41. 387 U.S., at 26.
42. Quoted in *McKeiver* 403 U.S., at 540.
43. 403 U.S., at 544–45.
44. Ibid., at 543.
45. Ibid., at 545.
46. Ibid., at 550.
47. 387 U.S., at 18.
48. Ibid., at 36.
49. Ibid., at 47.
50. *The Challenge of Crime in a Free Society,* p. 85.
51. 403 U.S., at note 4.
52. Ibid., at note 5.
53. *The Effectiveness of Delinquency Prevention Programs,* in U.S. Children's Bureau Publication No. 350 (1954), p. 46.
54. Ibid., p. 50.
55. "Criminal Justice, Legal Values, and the Rehabilitative Ideal," reprinted in Goldstein and Goldstein, op. cit., pp. 279–80.
56. Eileen Younghusband, "The Dilemma of the Juvenile Court," *Social Service Review,* XXXII, No. 1 (March 1959), p. 20.
57. Schultz and Cohen, "Isolationism in Juvenile Court Jurisprudence," in *Pursuing Justice for the Child,* p. 39.
58. "Juvenile Justice and the National Crime Commissions," in *Pursuing Justice for the Child,* p. 291.
59. The Court quotes the commission's assessment in *Gault,* 387 U.S., at note 23.
60. *Struggle for Justice: A Report on Crime and Punishment in America* (New York, 1971), pp. 43, 145.
61. Schultz and Cohen, op. cit., p. 40.
62. See, for example, Matza, *Delinquency and Drift,* p. 27.
63. *The Challenge of Crime in a Free Society,* p. 85.
64. 387 U.S., at note 26.
65. Quoted in Orman Ketcham and Monrad Paulsen, *Cases and Materials Relating to Juvenile Courts* (New York, 1967), pp. 422–23.
66. Sol Rubin, "The Legal Character of Juvenile Delinquency," in Rose Giallombardo, ed., *Juvenile Delinquency: A Book of Readings* (New York, 1966), p. 27.
67. Geoffrey Hazard, Jr., "The Jurisprudence of Juvenile Delinquency," in *Pursuing Justice for the Child,* p. 8.
68. The work of Edwin Schur leads this school of thought: see *Radical Nonintervention: Rethinking the Delinquency Problem* (Englewood Cliffs, N.J., 1973).

INDEX

Juvenile Psychopathic Institute,
83
Juvenile Record, 16–17

Katz, Jay, 73, 75
Kent v. U.S., 148, 150
Kohs, Samuel, 112–13
Korn, Richard, 122

labor, child, 27
land, use of, 7, 11–12
Lathrop, Julia, 31–2, 45, 138
law, contributing-to-delinquency,
   36; criminal, 17, 32–3, 35, 37,
   45, 55, 57, 63, 66, 71–2, 74–5,
   95, 137, 145, 149, 152, 160;
   enforcement of, 60–2; juvenile
   court, 36–7, 43–6, 53–4, 63, 66–
   8, 70, 72, 74, 81, 87, 159–60
Lemert, Edwin, 134
Lenroot, Katherine, 82, 88–92, 94
Lewis, Henry King, 29
Lindsey, Benjamin, 30, 36, 39, 48,
   52, 76, 80, 87, 138
literacy tests, 12
Lombroso, Cesare, 21–2, 24
Los Angeles, juvenile court of, 96,
   103
Louisville, Ky., probation officers
   in, 78
Lubove, Roy, 49, 101, 118
Lundberg, Emma, 90, 94, 139

Mack, Julian, 43, 65, 96
Mackay, Henry, 126–7
McKeiver et al. v. Pennsylvania,
   148, 150, 153–4, 156–7
M'Naghten case, 73
Maryland, workmen's compensa-
   tion law of, 10
Massachusetts, juvenile laws in,
   35–6; and minimum wages, 10
Matza, David, 23, 132–3, 135
mens rea, 73–4
Merton, Robert K., 131
Michigan Supreme Court, 67
Mill v. Brown, 71
Miller, Walter B., 129

modernization, 14–15, 54
Morgan, J. P., 8
Morrison, William Douglas, 24
Murphy, J. Prentice, 94

National Commission on Law
   Observance, 138; Report of the
   Causes of Crime of, 127
National Conference of Charities
   and Correction, 25–6, 53, 64, 75,
   116
National Conference of Social
   Work, 139
National Council on Crime and
   Delinquency, 144
National Probation Association,
   95, 139, 142
natural resources, 7, 12
neutralization, 133–5
New Jersey Conference of Charities
   and Correction, 80
New York, houses of refuge in, 19
New York Court of Appeals, 151
New York Family Court Act, 144
New York State Probation Com-
   mission, 86
New York School of Social Work,
   107
Newlands Reclamation Act, 11

Ohio Bureau of Juvenile Research,
   117
Ohio Humane Society, 42
One Thousand Delinquents, 93
Owen-Glass Act of 1914, 11

Packer, Herbert, 58, 60, 62
panics: 1819, 6; 1837, 6; 1893, 8,
   54
parens patriae, 63–6, 68, 71–2,
   135, 148–50
parole, abolition of, 79
Pedagogical Seminary, 27, 30
penal system, 35; *see also kinds of
   institutions*
penitentiaries, 18–19, 26, 33
Pennsylvania, juvenile court act
   of, 67; Supreme Court of, 153–4